MIND
DRIVING

MIND DRIVING

NEW SKILLS FOR STAYING ALIVE ON THE ROAD

STEPHEN HALEY

This edition first published in Great Britain in 2006
© Safety House 2006

First published by:
Safety House Publishing, a subsidiary of Safety House Ltd
Safety House, Beddington Farm Lane, Croydon CR0 4XZ

Safety House Ltd Reg. No. 5316585
www.driving.org

DIA Mail Order code 0128
Mail order hotline: 020 8665 5253

ISBN   1-873371-16-0
          978-1-873371-16-9

Text design and typesetting by Stephen Haley
Jacket design by Steven Russell

Printed and bound by Crossprint Ltd, Newport, Isle of Wight, UK.

Papers used by Safety House Publishing are natural, recyclable products made from wood
grown in sustainable forests. The manufacturing processes conform to the environmental
regulations of the country of origin.

Foreword

This totally new approach to driving skill and improving our road safety record has been desperately needed for a long time. Never before has the focus been put so squarely on to a driver's thinking - which is where danger or safety really starts.

Year after year on the roads around the globe 1.25 million people die, and more than 20 million are seriously injured. It is the most colossal worldwide carnage, which must be addressed. And one of the most effective ways is to advance our understanding about the skills that are actually needed for safe driving.

This book does exactly that - and in a superbly practical fashion. Its unique approach makes us think, and think hard, about the way we drive and how safely we do it. Every driver and teacher of driving should read it. There are over 40 million licence holders in the United Kingdom alone, most of whom take driving far too lightly, with only one per cent of drivers opting for further training after taking the basic test.

Mind Driving takes us step by step through a modern approach to driving and driver training. Crucially, it shows very clearly the *thinking skills* that have previously been so difficult to explain. It is essential that drivers and trainers update their knowledge and techniques, and acquire the skills that today's hectic roads and traffic demand.

Reading this book should definitely change the way we drive and make us safer, and without question it can help reduce the huge toll of fatalities and injuries on the roads.

Graham R J Fryer
Chief Executive
Driving Instructors Association
Safety House Group

About the author

Stephen loves driving, and is passionate about enjoying it safely. But he has an unlikely background for writing this book - a 30 year career in a multinational company, IBM. During that time, his work has spanned the diverse fields of finance, marketing and skill development, although he has a degree in engineering.

The single thread that connected this career, though, was the reputation for taking a wide and lateral view - and resolving deep seated problems by seeing them differently.

So when his children reached motoring age, and he tried to explain to them the art of "experienced driving", it triggered a fascinating challenge - to discover what really defines the true skill of safe driving.

As the journey unfolded, Stephen built a strong network of experts across many fields of road safety. And the enthusiasm from this group grew quickly as it became clear what was taking shape. When the full set of skills had been defined and developed a website was created to give the total new approach a much wider audience, and this generated even more positive feedback - especially from driving trainers and very experienced drivers.

A key influence throughout this project were some principles that Stephen had seen work well in skill development:
- clearly defined skills are much easier to learn
- skills can only work well together if they genuinely fit well together
- good teaching should inspire more learning.

His driving experience spans 40 years and about 700 thousand miles. Along the way he has taken a number of training courses and passed an advanced test. He describes his driving style as "purposeful", because every action is deliberate and with specific reason. He also rode motorcycles for some years, and is still a regular cyclist.

Stephen can be contacted at: steve@skilldriver.org

What people say

"There are lots of good ideas here, and a new approach like this is urgently needed. Driver skill is still the biggest untapped potential in road safety."

Kevin Delaney, Head of Traffic and Road Safety RAC Foundation, formerly head of Metropolitan Police Traffic Department

"This book sets new standards which should not only be applauded, but should be recommended reading for all motorists as the further learning they need after the test."

Viscount Jan Simon, a Deputy Speaker of the House of Lords. IAM, RoSPA Gold Class, DIAmond Advanced Motorist; passed the Police Class 1 driver test. President of the DIA.

"It is intriguing to see an approach to driving skill that is so different. The Sense of Danger model is very simple, and really does work. For any driver, these new skills will change the way they think - and definitely build better safety."

Andrew Howard, Head of Road Safety, AA Motoring Trust

"What a refreshing and open-minded insight into driving skill! Packed with new ideas, this really captures the thought patterns to bring out any driver's best ability. This is how to stop crashes, and get the death rate falling again as it should be."

Pete Garvey, corporate Defensive Driving instructor and consultant, RoSPA and DIAmond Advanced examiner, ex-police Class 1 instructor

"This is a terrific book. It makes you rethink the things you take for granted, and it will be particularly useful to those instructors involved in Pass Plus and Advanced test training."

Colin O'Connell, Chief Examiner DIAmond Advanced Motorists

"This is absolutely outstanding! Exactly the breakthrough and fresh thinking on skills that will make safer drivers - at all levels. With this approach there is no longer any excuse for neglecting driver skills as the most important element in road safety."

Mark McArthur-Christie, RoSPA Gold Class driver, IAM Local Group leader, ABD Director of Policy

"This is brilliant! Especially the explanation of the thinking processes, and the focus on active risk management. Crashes are caused by people, and these are exactly the skills to help drivers prevent them."

Graham Ellis, Crash Investigator, 20 years

"Mind Driving provides a unique insight into the process of safe driving. In years to come it will be remembered as a milestone in the history of road safety. Much of the content is known to the safest drivers but has never previously been seen in print. This is essential reading for drivers and anyone involved in road safety."

Paul Smith, founder of the Safe Speed road safety campaign

"This is excellent and I strongly recommend it to all drivers. It should be compulsory reading for all driving instructors - and Members of Parliament!"

Philip Cornes, IAM Senior Observer, RoSPA Gold Class 12yrs, ADI retired

"Congratulations on an excellent book! Shows a superb grasp of where the accountability lies, and encourages the driver to take full responsibility for what happens."

Eugene Herbert, Managing Director, RAC Driving Solutions, South Africa

Contents

Introduction

a personal story

Our two children made me write this book. Not deliberately, they didn't even know. But they were the reason it started. It is about how to prevent collisions on the road by taking active control of risk. This new approach to driving skill starts with a personal story.

How it began

Some years ago, our family summer holidays fell into a pattern. We packed up the car and spent three weeks camping across Europe, venturing deep into the heart of the continent. I was the driver, partly because I enjoyed it, but also because my wife is an excellent navigator in strange places!

Much of our motoring was at high speed on the big roads, covering the distance between stops.

As we cruised the hours away down sun-baked tarmac and concrete, I could feel the children watching how I made the car do what it did. And at times they cast an eager eye on the speedo too, as children will.

One summer this struck me more than usual. "When I get my car..." had entered the family banter, as the lure of independence hovered on the horizon. Our son was now 15 years old, and just itching to have a go at driving. Our daughter was 13, with a fondness for the most extreme fairground rides she could find.

And so, as I imagined the day they climbed behind the wheel, a new worry was looming into focus.

The problem was simple:

> they were getting a totally false impression of driving, and it was coming from me!

It looks so easy, often even casual. Just point the car, push a pedal or two, and off it goes. Like a magic carpet. And going fast? Well, that looks like the easiest part. The driver has even less to do, and other traffic seems to know just how to stay clear too. No problem at all.

The question was how to fix this notion. It is logical that non-drivers imagine the task to be what they see being done - steering, pedals, gears, etc. Yet all experienced drivers know that this leaves out a huge and crucial piece. Which is, of course, the invisible <u>thinking</u> part. Just as when you look at a car, you can't see what makes the wheels go round. It's all hidden underneath. So the "secret" was a whole churning universe in my head that my two eager young cherubs knew nothing about.

But it would be meaningless to tell these aspiring young motorists about some crucial thinking that they couldn't see - unless I could also say what it was. And at that stage I didn't know. After more than two decades of driving high mileage, it was still just a busy jumble. Clearly, though, their L-test training would not cover it. This side of driving has always been assumed to be somehow absorbed later.

It became clear, after pondering this for a while, that:

driving is actually a <u>mainly</u> thinking task.

The physical actions simply carry out what the thinking has carefully decided to do. So safety or danger is in the <u>decisions</u> about what to make the car do - well before the action is taken. This makes driving a "thinking task with physical involvement", not the other way round. It is a bit like chess, where the pieces must be physically moved in order to play, but the outcome lies in the mental skill. The key is that:

when the <u>thinking</u> is right, the right actions will follow.

That was the first breakthrough, though it just moved the problem on a step. The issue then became how to unravel all this thinking activity. The more I dwelled on it, the more this seemed to be the holy grail of safe driving. The thing that would somehow define real competence.

A stream of questions erupted from this. What exactly <u>are</u> the decisions we take, and how do we make <u>good</u> ones? What <u>is</u> safety, and how can we <u>control</u> it? Indeed, what makes <u>danger</u>, and how can we <u>predict</u> it? What are the <u>skills</u>, and the best way to <u>learn</u> them? How can we tell <u>how good</u> they are? And so on…

That was quickly quite a tumbling shopping list! But all had to be answered. Yet none are as obvious as we want them to be, otherwise there would be far less crashes. The very least I wanted to do was capture and explain the instincts of very experienced safe drivers. Especially important was to accelerate the learning of novices through the minefield of their early years behind the wheel.

The toughest problem of all, though, seemed to be that the thinking skills are so much more difficult to examine than the physical ones we can watch being used.

Easy answers

Hoping for some easy answers, I began to ask drivers I knew a simple question: "How do you make sure you drive safely?". They all had long years of hard won experience behind them. Some were very high mileage professional drivers, most of whom must avoid crashing to keep their job.

The usual response was a hesitant: "Er... good question...!", struggling with something that sounded as if it should be easy. This was followed by something like, "When you drive as many miles as I do, you get an instinct", or "By thinking about everything all of the time", or "You get a sixth sense. It just becomes second nature".

Through their discomfort, this still confirmed three things. First, the answer was definitely in their thinking. Also, it was about a lot of things happening together. And lastly, they couldn't explain it! In fact:

the almost mystic theme seemed to say that it could not be defined at all.

Importantly, though, no one said they relied on car handling skills and following the regulations. They all took the question at a higher level than that. Critically, for example, the Highway Code does not contain topics like observation, anticipation, hazard recognition, risk assessment, or learning from experience. Yet they are clearly vital. Neither does it include a list of the skills needed to be safe.

At about this time I had my first Defensive Driving session - with an instructor who also trained police drivers. I recall it vividly. We met in the office, and walked to a coffee machine exchanging small talk. After a while he asked, "So what do you expect me to be telling you today?". I had one sure expectation. "Not to drive so fast", I said, trying not to sound too guilty. He took his cup carefully from the machine and said softly, "...and what good would that do?". I was stunned, and my attention rocketed. Without the recurring headline to "Slow Down!", this would be very interesting! Looking back, it was the most effective, and enjoyable, training day in my driving career. It was an eye-opener in many ways. Actually, quite inspiring. And the reason is clearer with hindsight. The focus was always on coaching me to make better decisions of my own, rather than trying to make them for me with instructions about what to do. And the speed question? Well, that is just one of the decisions we make - matching it to everything else. Sometimes we took it down a little, and sometimes up a bit. That day sparked some very new thinking. A key piece of the story was definitely in:

making our own skilful decisions.

A while later, I heard a police driver on television say, "It takes at least 100,000 miles to make an experienced driver". It sounded true. But waiting for so many miles to pass totally fails the many youngsters who don't make it that far. Also, many older drivers have clearly learnt little from their long experience anyway. So, why does it take so long? And why do some learn more than others? To call it different aptitude just evades the vital question. The challenge is how to get 100,000 miles of experience, and even more, into a much shorter span.

It's about risk

Having found no easy answers, I was still struggling to see what all the thinking activity was about, and how it created safety. So I resorted to the dictionary - and found the answer. "Safety" is defined as "freedom from danger". It exists only as the <u>absence</u> of danger, like quiet is the absence of sound.

So nothing increases safety directly, instead it acts to reduce a danger. And this is not just playing with words.

A focus squarely on "danger" itself will force a much better grasp of how it works and how to influence it, than if the goal is expressed as "safety".

From that, it didn't take long to realise that handling danger on the road happens in four parts, that work in a cycle:

- <u>spotting</u> where the danger is
- <u>assessing</u> how serious it is
- <u>deciding</u> what to do
- <u>taking</u> the necessary action.

But these are also the steps in any basic risk management process. So this tells us that:

safe driving is, in fact, an exercise in
actively managing risk.

Suddenly, the thinking clicked into shape! This is what my churning thoughts had been doing all along. Even more, this meant that the total act of driving itself should be explainable as a process of how risk is handled through the stages.

The spotlight now swung squarely on to "risk" - what causes it, how to assess it, and how to control it. And clearly, any answers would need to be both complete enough to be realistic, <u>and</u> simple enough to be useful in our driving. This promised to be difficult. What immediately seemed unlikely, though, was that one thing could emerge as a single solution for handling risk. Life is more complex than that, especially on the road.

However, this was still all too academic. The whole quest would only be worthwhile if specific <u>practical</u> skills could be found. That was the only meaningful goal to have.

Alongside this, two further things stood out in my mind as essential to explain. The first was how to <u>prevent</u> danger from occurring. This is more critical than just reacting when it becomes obvious, and holds the secret to keeping risk very low. And the second thing was about danger caused by <u>others</u>. It is well known that:

almost all collisions could be avoided by
<u>any</u> of the road-users involved,
if only someone had seen it coming!

So being safe includes avoiding someone else's crash too, and refusing to be a victim. This is a vital survival skill, that we must believe we can do something about.

This book

By now you will know that this book is unlike any other you will find on driving - and it will feel different too. It is fully centred on the activity in your head, and this is a radical approach that is overdue in modern driving.

The aim is to dramatically boost the control that you have over the inevitable dangers you face on the road, especially the ones created by other people. And to do that by getting right to the core of how you deal with risk. This in itself marks a major breakthrough over the traditional view of the skills involved.

It is intended for nearly all drivers, from those who are a few thousand miles after passing the test, up to those with very long experience. But the purpose is not to help beginners through the test. Instead, it kicks in when the old adage:

"you really learn to drive after passing the test"

leaves the puzzling void of what that means, and how to do it.

There is nothing here, though, that is harder than the basic training - just very different. And there is a lot more to gain in real control of danger, and in clear skills to be proud of.

You will learn simple "eyes and brain" skills, which are even more vital than the ones in your "hands and feet". And discover how to have very high control over events - with much less stress and frustration too. It is a deeply personal approach to help you, as an individual, improve your survival - and enjoyment - on the road.

Especially, there are no traditional instructions that tell you exactly what to do. That would be just a faithful mimic of the books already on the shelves. Instead, the focus is on helping drivers to think differently and make better decisions of their own. This is how to achieve real control over situations that are complex and unique, and unlike textbook examples.

This is still, though, not an instant magic cure for all hazards. Nothing ever could be. So you should:

expect to build your skills over time.

No one can pick up a book on Friday evening and emerge from the weekend as a born-again motorist.

A few other points:
- The focus is solely on safety. Driving to save cost or the environment is not covered. Whatever their merits, the solid anchor in safety comes first
- The term "road user" includes all vehicles and people on the road, plus any who might join them, such as cars in driveways and children on a footpath
- The points emphasised in bold text lines are coloured broadly to indicate:
  - **red for an alert to danger**
  - **blue for a general point**
  - **green for increased safety**
- Lastly, while some conventional views may be robustly challenged, take nothing to suggest or condone breaking the law. Driving legally is fundamental too.

And what value can any book be? Well, certainly no book can <u>make</u> you an expert driver - but it definitely can show you how to make yourself one!

As an ancient Zen proverb says:

> **"When the pupil is ready, then the teacher will appear".**

It means simply that when we want to learn, we will find a way to do it. How true.

So ultimately, this book is as much about enabling and encouraging a learning process as it is about specific knowledge and skills.

Certainly, taking responsibility for your own skill is already a shrewd decision.

This book is set out in readily digestible sections to be easy to read at any pace, and to refer back to later. And remember, with this or any other book, that you are the driver in control of your vehicle, and must therefore make sure you use the information safely.

For my own part, my understanding of driving has been profoundly changed by the process of writing this book. The fact that it proved to be such a radical approach made it even more worthwhile, and from an early stage it took on a life of its own. But one of the hardest things has been to write a <u>practical</u> book about <u>thinking</u>!

Welcome to **Mind Driving**, I hope you enjoy it, and that it serves you well.

Part 1: Defining the skills

Part 1: Defining the skills

> <u>Key points</u>: - **Control and safety can only be increased with the <u>right</u> skills.**
>
> - **And there are more than the obvious ones.**

You probably think you know exactly what driving is - that it is plainly obvious in what you do.

But if you asked ten people to describe it, they would give ten different answers.

And all would leave a lot out.

This exposes a vital problem right at the beginning. There are many different notions of the task, and far more actually going on than meets the eye!

If your ten people are an average bunch, they will tell you a lot about the rules to follow and what they do with their hands and feet.

But they will probably not say much about:

what is happening in their head.

That is, how they, as the driver, <u>decide</u> what to do...

This is the largely unknown part - the elusive thinking that really determines whether someone is safe.

So there is a lot of uncovering to do before we can talk confidently about gaining useful skills.

Learning the <u>right</u> things is vital to making a difference, especially when there is more to the task than it seems on the surface.

In the next few pages we will identify the skills of driving in a way that has not been done before - examining the total task, and concentrating on how you <u>make your decisions</u>.

You may be surprised to see it all laid out. We will see:

> <u>why</u> the skills are what they are, and how they work together.

This gives essential preparation for **Part 2: Gaining the Skills** that forms the main body of the book later.

Tracking down the skills is divided into the three stages that follow:

- **Surrounding issues**
  - briefly opens some wider topics around driver behaviour and road safety. The topics strongly affect people's opinions on driving, and so form an ideal backdrop to thinking about skills.

- **The Driving Process**
  - uncovers the elements of the driving task, and how they fit together - especially the thinking parts.

- **Skills and the Learning Curve**
  - reveals a set of eight specific skills that make up safe driving, and plots them through five stages of competence.

1.1 Surrounding issues

> **Key point:** - There are many wider issues that influence how we think about our ability to drive.

There is no insulating vacuum around driving skill. Many wider issues, in motoring and beyond, strongly affect what people expect from their driving - and also what they think about how well they do it. So these issues provide a very valid and broadening backdrop to exploring our skills.

It may sound like a saying from an ancient Eastern guru, but it is true that:

"the view you take of a problem sets a frame for the answers you are able to find."

Ideas are often limited by taking a "symptoms-only" view. This contains the most obvious signs of a problem, and actions that aim at symptoms are generally easier to find and to execute than ones that tackle root causes.

But stabbing at symptoms is the most universally futile way of dealing with problems, even though it might satisfy the urgency to "just do something!". Because in reality:

you are unlikely to genuinely fix something if the underlying causes are left intact.

This does not say ignore symptoms, of course. They often need urgent attention. But if no more is done, then it is a poor solution - and probably an endless task too.

So in this chapter, the main aim is to open and stir your thoughts. And when controversial points are made, how far you agree with them is less important than provoking some thinking, and bringing the issues to the front of your mind. Some of the problems with traditional approaches to road safety are rooted in these issues.

Certainly, history shows that conventional wisdom can get bogged down, and act as "guide rails" for itself.

This holds back progress, until fresh ideas and lateral thinking come along to break through the gridlock. And this may come from unexpected sources.

Also, as often happens with complex and deep-seated problems, many aspects of road safety would be easier to fix if only we didn't have to start from where we are!

So another purpose here is to:

*recognise the world the way it is, rather than
just wishing it were different.*

The topics are kept brief below, so as to not slow the pace at this stage.

1.1.1 Who cares about road safety?

It is hard to admit, but as a society, our interest in road safety is quite weak. Certainly, local groups are vocal on their own issues, and people express concern if prompted in a survey. There is also intense suffering and anguish for anyone who is close to a tragedy. But on the broader stage, the collective mind of the public is more preoccupied elsewhere.

Typically, concerns of the nation are dominated by big issues such as health, education, violent crime, employment, etc. Which means that:

road safety comes a long way down the list.

Even rail and air crashes attract far more attention than those on the road - with a tiny fraction of the annual casualties. Motorists themselves also get far more agitated over issues like congestion and fuel prices than safety. So combating overcrowded roads may feature prominently in a political manifesto, but not reducing casualties.

This shows a curious public tolerance for road casualties alongside other issues. But whether this is logical or right is not the question here. More important is that we can't expect, or wait, for it to change. And therefore:

*the best strategy for your <u>own</u> safety is in your own hands
- by increasing your driving skill.*

1.1.2 Casualties in context

Despite the amount of time we spend on the road, few people know just how safe or dangerous it is to drive. We do not get the information in the right way. In fact, there are many greater risks in life than using the roads. Suicides and accidents in the home are each greater causes of death, and even these are totally dwarfed by the results of tobacco, alcohol or obesity.

However, although it is very rare to see a crash happen, the average driving career in Great Britain has:

ten collisions that are worth an insurance claim.

They vary widely in severity, of course, and bring a 50% chance of any individual being injured on the road at some point in their life, and also a 1-in-200 chance of being killed. Perhaps this now sounds like a threat that is worth protecting yourself against.

This is especially true when you realise that causing any injury at all to the occupants of a modern car is likely to take a pretty severe crash - possibly totally writing off the vehicle.

Deep in the casualty figures is a lot of information that might help focus people's attention if they knew it. For example, in Great Britain (2004 data):

- three-quarters of all road deaths are male
- nearly half of the deaths are not inside a vehicle, but are walking or on two wheels
- 45% of deaths happen in the hours of darkness - even with much less traffic
- 70% of total injuries happen in speed limits of 40mph or less
- motorways are the safest roads, carrying 19% of traffic with 5% of the deaths.

We can note too that road casualties hit a much younger mix of people than the other major dangers. This matters because we are more sensitive to harm that befalls children and young people.

Most alarming, though, is the overall trend in fatalities. After a strong and steady decline since 1970, the falling line suddenly stalled in the mid-1990s, and remained flat for a decade.

And this happened even though underlying benefits were still coming through each year from safer new cars, road improvements and medical advances.

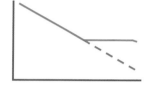

But there is no agreement on what prevented further reductions for so long.

Although 2004 saw a welcome decline, the death rate by that time was about 35% higher than the long term trend line - which is some 1200 fatalities per year.

There is a lot of catching up to do in these numbers:

if only someone knew what to do differently now!

1.1.3 Can statistics help?

Ideally, collisions would all be analysed into exactly how they happened, and then recorded into reliable figures to show us how to avoid everything that causes them.

But life is far from that simple. Most crashes defy attempts to be sure about the real root cause.

Even in a classic rear shunt, how can we split the responsibility between going too fast, travelling too close, and not paying attention?

And how can we say which one would have best prevented it?

Usually, crashes are caused by a combination of things that happen together. So while the result of a crash is easy to see, being certain about the cause is notoriously difficult. This presents clear problems in compiling and using the statistics, and despite a very large volume of research around the world:

there are many different conclusions
about what causes crashes.

However, for anyone who works at trying to reduce the casualties, the task is always urgent, which creates a strong pressure to know why things happen, and what to do. The same pressure also demands to see rapid results from any action that is taken. Unfortunately though, the most statistically significant point seems to be the lack of agreement on what the figures can really tell us.

This calls into question whether the data is able to provide answers at the level that people need. And the danger is that if the numbers are wielded beyond their ability, then needless casualties might easily result from taking the wrong action.

The most reliable sense of danger should always be:

the driver's own skilful assessment of the situation.

1.1.4 Risk - who is in control?

Some people might prefer that it were not so, but risk is part of life. And so therefore is risk-taking to some degree. As soon as we get out of bed in the morning there is inescapable danger lurking in everything we do. We could trip over the cat on the stairs, get robbed in the street, buy a second-hand car, or start a new job. Depending on your disposition:

risk is either a harsh reality of life,
or the essence of the opportunity to live.

In truth, we do need risk in our life. It is a vital stimulation that keeps us alert, challenged and engaged in what we are doing.

This dates back over thousands of generations to our primeval ancestors whose lives were a constant struggle to prevail over danger just to stay alive.

Even more, learning and practising the mastery of risk has played a crucial role in how mankind thrived and became the supreme creature on the planet.

Indeed, "nothing ventured, nothing gained" has shaped the path of human development.

And now, beneath the trappings of a modern world, the instincts that were forged in that dim and distant past remain intact. The basic human material is the same, and enjoying an active and rewarding life still has the need for a balanced experience of risk. So if we seek safety by trying to banish completely such a fundamental trait, we are destined to fail. It would be like trying to control a car by just pretending it is not moving. The die is already cast, and:

no one is going to re-engineer human nature.

Neither should anyone encourage a belief that life can be made risk-free. It is reckless to assume that people would accept the blandness of such an existence. Certainly, there is always a level of precaution that is sensible to take. But beyond that, the need to face up to risk is an essential part of our daily routine.

And we will always be dealing with a <u>balance</u>, neither being reckless nor trying to eradicate risk altogether.

Crucially, no one should live in fear of life itself.

That would succumb to being a "prisoner to risk", who does nothing for fear of everything.

So where does driving sit in this sea of life, full of inevitable risks? Well, for most of us, it is simply the most hazardous thing that we regularly do. Danger is a natural consequence of moving around, and we need the ability to cope with it well.

Nevertheless, do not imagine that focusing hard on risk will condemn your driving to being sedentary, nervous or dull. Quite the reverse. The aim is to:

discover how to control the risk, not to shrink timidly
so that it controls you.

The expert driver has the skills and a driving style that are safe, yet also purposeful, confident and enjoyable at the same time. By contrast, recklessness <u>and</u> over-caution are both a surrender of full control by failing to understand what is happening. As we saw before, safe driving is an exercise in <u>active</u> risk management. And this should be the common thread that runs through everything we think and do behind the wheel.

However, we start with a picture that is confused by the way most of us already think about risk. It even contains its own contradictions as we all do things like:

- react to the word "risk" as if it means being reckless
- pretend that risk does not exist, and avoid responsibility for it
- let small risks stop us doing normal things
- become dependent on being warned about dangers
- deny that risk serves a purpose in helping us to function well
- believe that protecting children completely from risk is good for them
- tell other people what level of risk they should be happy with
- use safety measures as an opportunity to be more careless.

Especially important is the effect on children of trying to spoon-feed them safety, and squeeze them into a risk-free existence.

By depriving them of the freedom to experience danger and learn how to handle it, they lack the skills needed later to assess and control risk for themselves.

It is unreal, and they are more frail when their world opens up, with no choice but to face life squarely and independently - and make their own decisions.

No matter how you see risk:

the priority is surely to control your own destiny.

It is not enough to be swept along by events and just hope to get by. On the road, this means both controlling the danger you create, and also protecting yourself from everyone else. This is the very simple, but powerful, idea of "self-destiny".

Of course, the sensation of risk is a subjective feeling - not an objective fact. And telling someone what to do has no effect on how much risk they are happy to take. So unless people genuinely <u>want</u> to be safer, they will always frustrate the efforts of anyone who tries to do it for them.

And it becomes clearer now that mastering risk will involve somehow cooperating with the natural need for stimulation, rather than trying to eliminate it.

Firstly, that will need a good grasp of the causes of risk, and then knowing how to assess and control the danger to achieve a "low risk bubble" around you. Especially important is to recognise specifically when and how you incur risks that are higher than you intended - including the threats to you that are caused by others.

And finally, as your skills grow, it must be in a way that avoids spilling over into a new source of overconfidence. That would simply defeat the whole achievement!

1.1.5 The role of government - carrot or stick?

The biggest role in road safety is played by government.

Their control stretches across all aspects of motoring, from the design and maintenance of highways and vehicles, to driving standards, traffic law and policing.

This gives both:
> **the opportunity and the responsibility to have the best influence on how road users regard safety.**

There are striking differences, though, in the way that governments tackle their role in different countries.

Two points stand out in particular:

- **Trust**
    - Whether people trust their government, and believe they are told the truth is critical to <u>everything</u>. In road safety, it determines whether people will listen to advice from official sources.
    - Motives must also be clear, and safety measures must be kept separate from those that have environmental aims or seek to discourage motoring.
    - Even more widely, any lack of trust rubs off firmly on the general level of respect for law and order.
- **Policy Balance**
    - Law enforcement and driver training are in many ways alternatives to each other, since both are aimed at creating safe behaviour. And the balance between them is a matter of policy choice.
    - However, law enforcement is a "socially negative" option, based on compulsion, surveillance and penalties. Whereas driver training is "socially positive" - empowering and raising valuable skills. It is a classic "carrot versus stick" choice, that strikes to the heart of the sort of society you want to live in.

- But in reality, there is no substitute for the skills of the driver - even the combined efforts of the car and highway designers, law-makers and police. Because the driver is the only person who is on the spot, making judgements and in control.

In any country, scanning the local media for a while will show up any concerns with the policies being pursued.

In Great Britain some deep worries emerged after the mid-1990's. And since about 2000 politicians have talked increasingly of the need to win back public trust. Most visible has been the level of concern about the large sums of money raised by speed camera fines.

Even more, for the aim of reducing casualties, it has been strange that:

> the true Education element of road safety has been
> given the least opportunity to contribute.

Certainly, it seems too harsh to blame drivers for not having skills that they have not been shown. But experts in driver training have struggled to move a government strategy that looks increasingly like pushing ever harder on a door that probably opens the other way.

1.1.6 The speed question - the real killer?

Using the roads is an integral part of modern life, and it is vital that we can do so both safely and efficiently. Within this, every driver has an absolute responsibility to always use an appropriate speed.

This sounds simple enough, but is confused by there being:

> a broad lack of agreement on how speed relates to danger.

Strongly opposing views are held by different people, for different reasons. And this is now firmly entrenched as one of the most controversial aspects of motoring safety. But the fact that it touches such a raw nerve makes it vital to acknowledge the issue squarely.

Even more crucially for us, the way that drivers think about speed fundamentally alters the way they think about exercising control over their vehicle.

Some countries have formed their road safety policy around a firm belief that slower traffic speeds will significantly cut casualties.

This includes Great Britain, where since the early 1990's the "Speed Kills" philosophy has been at the centre of road safety strategy. And enforcing speed limits, using laser and camera technology, dramatically increased the number of speeding convictions to over two million per year.

From the safety viewpoint, this strategy is sustained by two things.
First is a gut feeling that it "should" work. After all, the slower you go the easier it is to stop, and slower crashes should also be less violent. And second are figures from some camera sites that have shown dramatic reductions in casualties.

Against this though, as we saw before, is the disturbing fact that:

at the national level the death rate has remained flat.

This is the ultimate test, and is at the crux of the issue. Therefore, serious concerns have been growing not only among individuals, but motoring organisations and some senior ranks of the police too. In fairness, many of the worries were raised much earlier as the strategy was taking shape.

The concerns are well documented, and include:

- **Randomness:** Most of the effect recorded at camera sites has been found to be simply the continuation of random variations and natural trends in crash rates.

- **Worse trend:** As we saw before, the focus on speed has coincided with a sharply worse trend in road deaths, remaining flat rather than falling under the steady continuing effects of safer vehicles, improved roads and better medical care.

- **Speed limits:** Driving situations are far too varied to expect a speed limit to reflect actual levels of danger. Indeed, most serious crashes happen below the speed limits, not above them. The crucial point for us is that driving at a speed limit is <u>not</u> a skill, whereas deciding on a safe speed definitely is.

- **Inattention:** Everyone has an attention threshold, below which they become "under-loaded", and begin to disengage from what is happening. So attention tends to fall if a speed seems artificially low.

  Some argue further, that the focus on speed has diverted attention away from better safety actions - at both the policy level and for drivers behind the wheel. This includes placing less value on driving skill, and the possibility that drivers are led to prioritise watching their speedometer above searching for hazards.

- **Responsibility:** There is a powerful suggestion in rigid speed enforcement that responsibility for choosing an appropriate speed has transferred from the driver to the speed limit. This inevitably creates drivers who are less skilled at deciding what is actually safe for the situation - especially if a speed <u>lower</u> than the limit is needed.

- **Rare crashes:** Millions of people every day drive at speeds they deem to be safe but are over the limits, and yet crashes are still quite rare. So this constant practical experience casts doubt over a simple cause-and-effect connection. In fact, a serious-injury crash happens once in 8 million miles, which is 16 average driving careers. And even then, most are not blamed on going too fast. There must be something else very fundamental, it is argued, that turns normal speeds into a crash.

- **Safety in numbers:** It is not realistic to brand all drivers who go slightly over a speed limit as reckless and irresponsible. There are just too many of them - indeed "most" drivers. And the public is not that generally reckless. On the contrary, society is becoming much more averse to risk - even to the extent of losing the ability to cope with it.

- **Respect for the law:** In a leading democracy, defining lawful behaviour should include the normal careful actions of the adult majority. So then, good laws achieve a high level of voluntary compliance. But against this standard, speed limits stand out as an exception. Uniquely in the justice system, speed limits are broken every day by probably more people than vote in a general election. Such a vast disrespect carries weight, and people should not be criminalised on that scale.

Crucially too, for the social consequence, being prosecuted rarely triggers a sense of guilt. More often it provokes in the driver a resentment at what is seen as a senseless punishment that has nothing to do with safety. And since cameras detect only the numeric speed, not danger, the demand to be judged on safety has opened a rift of alienation between drivers and the law. Even more worrying for the future, is that this feeling will readily transmit in the home from parents to the children.

On top of that, the crushing irony is that the deliberately reckless drivers simply continue to ignore the law anyway - no matter how tough it gets on everyone else.

- **Cash machine:** Any strategy that gives the police part of the money raised in fines will always have a dramatic effect on public opinion. It inflames concerns about the large number of prosecutions, and creates the inescapable accusation that the speed enforcement has been designed as a callous tax on motorists.

It also inevitably positions the cameras as instruments of entrapment that have little to do with stopping dangerous driving. Most crucially, it distorts the objectives and motives of what should be a pure and clear safety measure. This has been tried and tested in different countries and found to be true.

Returning to the primary problem, the perspective of history is brutally clear. Something must be wrong when the death rate has stayed flat, instead of falling, during a decade of speed-centric safety policy. And the damaging social costs were definitely not factored into the balance either.

It seems reasonable to:

rethink the actual benefits and costs of a strategy
that carries such a very strict regime.

1.1.7 Limitations of rules

There are some formal rules and regulations that are very necessary in motoring just to keep us organised into sharing the same road network.

Alongside these are also many other rules given to drivers as general good practice. Examples are mirror-signal-manoeuvre, push-pull steering, being able to stop in the distance you can see to be clear, the two second gap, and so on. And this gives beginners a lot of help in avoiding being overwhelmed with decisions about what to do.

But the skill in a driving method that is built only on these rules is quite basic. And our grip on this crutch must be relaxed to raise our sights to a higher level.

It is like no longer relying on the stabiliser wheels on your first bicycle when you learned how to balance for yourself.

Indeed, relying too heavily on rules becomes reckless if it paralyses your proper thinking. Nothing can replace gaining and using better driving judgement, and:

we should never become "lost without rules".

Within this, there are specific reasons for venturing beyond being rule-dependent:

- to make your <u>own decisions,</u> and take <u>responsibility</u> for what you do
- to move the focus to your <u>thinking</u>, rather than concentrating on physical actions
- to see driving as a <u>constant flow</u>, not as a series of separate events
- to use the car's controls <u>naturally</u>, as an extension of your body.

In essence, this simply means acquiring the skills to think for yourself about what is safe. It has never been adequate to say, "Just stick to the rules, and you'll be all right". Certainly, whatever you are doing:

excellence does not come through rules alone.

So while some rules are definitely a necessary frame to build your skills around, they can never <u>be</u> your expertise - and especially not a substitute for it.

1.1.8 The problem with education

The general level of driver skills has a lot to answer for. Incompetence of some sort is responsible for nearly all casualties and damage on the road. The problem is that risk is poorly understood. And:

the reason can be traced directly back to the L-test.

The level of ability needed to get a full licence is very elementary. Only the basic skills are taught, and the focus is inevitably on the physical side of the task. But crucially, the novice gets no warning of the skills that are missing, nor any meaningful idea of learning after the test. Instead, they are taught to judge their performance against how well they follow the rules, and that the main thing needed after the test is just more practice.

This becomes a direct cause of overconfidence - especially in the young male group. It also gives no motivation to improve skills, and results in a wide range of inconsistent ability on the road as drivers make faltering progress over the years.

There can be no question that, although the L-test is the only legal requirement:

we need drivers to have far
more ability than that.

And this in itself admits the failure. Leaving novices to find their own way beyond their basic training lays the ground for a low standard to take root.

The huge piece missing, of course, is the thinking skills. And there will be a breakthrough when driver training reflects this. Drivers need to be shown clearly what these skills are, and how to put them into practice. No one disagrees that:

better thinking skills will prevent crashes.

But to inspire any learning at all is tough from where we are today. The wishful thinking, that drivers will find the missing skills themselves, has always been a hindrance in the traditional approach to training. Which then rebounds as a lack of belief in skill.

The path forward now needs a firmly restored faith in human ability, and for all the skills to be taught. It is vital to dispel the myths of the L-test, and to instil a clear sense of "elementary ability" at that level. The alternative of leaving the test as the only goal in a driver's mind is where the problem will continue to flourish.

Instead, a goal is needed that covers the full set of skills, and will last for a whole driving career. Only then will it achieve:

"lifelong learning" as a reality!

1.1.9 Enter the expert

In every activity there is a highest level of skill - the "expert". But to aim for it, we must first know what it is. In driving this has proved difficult, and no one has yet found a definition for the ultimate driving ability that has been generally accepted.

It is more than just being crash-free, otherwise beginners would be experts on the first day.

Neither does outstanding ability come from merely polishing up the basic training.

In truth, and in all fields of activity, the things that set experts apart are in the way they <u>think</u> and <u>learn</u>. And that is something we can change for ourselves - when we know how.

So what is "expert" in driving? And how can we express the point they have reached?

Any definition risks starting a heated debate, but we definitely need something tangible to work with. So for that purpose, let's take the bit between our teeth, and define an "expert safe driver" as one who:

"constantly manages risk, and maintains
a negligible threat of collision".

"Negligible" reflects that zero risk is an unrealistic aim. However, not only do these drivers have no collisions, there is also no reason to suspect they ever will - even one caused by someone else. Such is the mastery over risk. And the key is that they <u>anticipate</u> risk and control it early, rather than <u>reacting</u> to it later when it is a real threat.

Throughout this book the "expert" is used as a clear beacon to aim at. The intention is to show clearly how everyone can move solidly towards it from wherever they are today.

1.1.10 The process of learning

Failure to learn from experience is a powerful cause of poor driving skill. It acts in addition to the starting handicap in the standard of the L-test. But it is clear that:

<u>how</u> you try to learn is crucial in determining
the skills you end up with.

And there is a lot we can do to change how this happens.

It starts with finding a positive motivation. Everyone needs a reason to keep learning. And it is vital to find a process that is engaging and rewarding in itself, and also being able to enjoy what you are doing.

However, this is where the effect of heavy law enforcement and guilt-stirring safety campaigns can be discouraging. By sapping our enthusiasm for driving they also reduce the desire to do it well. And this presents a definite obstacle.

Also, your natural learning ability needs to be revived. One of the most powerful human strengths is that:

we are born with a huge and intuitive capacity to learn.

It works when we realise things for ourselves, rather than being closely instructed in what to do.

Although this learning ability is often suppressed in modern living, it is still the ideal way to gain from experience. It also builds the deeper and more flexible intuitive skills that are needed to reach high expertise.

Lastly, we must allow ourselves to admit errors freely, without the burden of criticism. Again, this is not the modern way. But it is decisive in being open to learning, rather than compelled to pretend that mistakes didn't happen, or don't matter.

This forms the core approach to learning used in this book.

1.1.11 In two minds - left and right brain

Continuing the point above on intuitive skills, the theory of left and right-sided functions in the brain connects surprisingly well with driving.

In this theory, the left-brain way of thinking operates well under instruction and when intently following rules. But in the right-brain mode are skills such as awareness, anticipation, intuition and relaxed concentration - all of which are crucial to skilled driving.

From this divide, the traditional approach to driving equates to treating it much as a left-brain task. Which might help to explain how an entire package of crucial skills are neglected. It also reveals how we fall into a "busy and frantic" style of driving that adds to stress and fatigue, rather than being calm and relaxed.

This shows from a different perspective what needs to change.

And if there is any "magic ingredient" to expert driving, it aligns very well with a need to:

bring the right-brain into play, and make it a whole-brain task.

Use your whole brain

1.1.12 And what it all means

A number of pointers emerge from the discussion above:

Your own expertise is the best safety measure
Your skills must deal with root causes of danger, not just its symptoms
Facing and controlling risk squarely should be at the core of your ability
Rules are not a substitute for gaining good skills
The scope of "driving skill" must embrace the whole task
Your learning journey after the test must be made very clear and tangible
The goal is to maintain negligible risk of collision
Learning is stronger when you enjoy what you are doing
Achieving high skill requires your natural learning processes
Errors must be seen as beacons for learning, not failures to be denied
The abilities called the "right-brain" functions are critical to safe driving

These are a useful background as we move on to explore what the specific skills of safe driving really are in the next two chapters.

1.2 The Driving Process

It is unlikely that you have ever thought of your driving as a "process". You just jump into the car and drive off.

Yet what happens down the road is exactly a process - a "continuous stream of events, with direct cause and effect". And by unravelling what that means, into explainable steps, we can find out more about the skills that are being used.

We already know that safety is determined in your thinking, not just what you do with the steering wheel and pedals.

So somehow we need to also see clearly things like:

- how <u>active risk management</u> is the core activity
- the critical role of your <u>decisions</u>
- how the thinking and physical parts <u>work together</u>
- driving as a fully <u>continuous</u> task
- how lots of things happen at the <u>same time</u>.

This will lay a strong foundation for much that comes later, so it is worth giving it some time. It will take, for example, no more than studying a few pages of the Highway Code.

Be clear, though, this is not trying to invent a new "driving system" or more lists of instructions to follow. It will simply reveal what is going on, and show more of what drivers are really doing. It is not even going to be something you need to learn. Just understanding the framework is enough, and being able to refer back to it readily later.

As we build the picture, ideally it will:

**show all the vital parts of driving, yet also be
easy to understand!**

1.2.1 Pieces of a jigsaw

> <u>Key point</u>: - The driving task has distinct activities that can be understood separately, and then as a whole.

To start understanding the driving task, we can take it in five pieces, like a jigsaw.

The pieces are:

- **the effect of what you know and believe**
- **choosing whether to drive**
- **sensing and understanding what is happening**
- **deciding what to do, and then doing it**
- learning from what happens.

Everything you do is there somewhere, though some pieces are simpler than others. But all the pieces are working all of the time, so as expected, there is a lot going on.

If you are impatient to ask <u>how</u> these things are done, that's a good sign. Though we must first be clearer about <u>what</u> they are. Moving on to "how" is what the whole of the much larger **Part 2: Gaining the Skills** is about later.

Each of the five activities above plays a distinct role in how people drive. And we will discuss them in turn under the headings:

Using Knowledge and Beliefs
Fitness Check
Observation Cycle
Control Cycle
Learning from Experience.

Read them below as <u>separate</u> pieces, then we will put them together into a total picture.

Using Knowledge and Beliefs

Your thinking processes are directed by what is in your memory. This sounds obvious, but it highlights some vital things that drivers need to get right.

Imagine it as the way you are "programmed" to drive - consciously and subconsciously. The linkage is very powerful, and control is exercised into your every perception, judgement and decision. It affects what things mean to you, how you think about them, and what you choose to do. Furthermore:

> **this programming can help safety or hinder it,**
> **but it is largely under your own control.**

So what is this "Knowledge and Beliefs"? Although everything in your head interacts in some way, four distinct elements are relevant for us here:

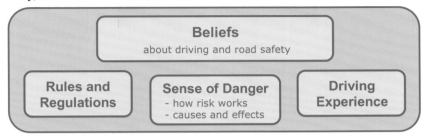

- **Beliefs:** are the inner personal beliefs that you hold about driving and road safety. They are formed in many ways, and will determine a driver's overall approach. Any problems with "attitude" will usually originate here.
- **Rules and Regulations:** are everything you remember about the Highway Code and motoring laws. This is a major part of basic training.
- **Sense of Danger:** is the way you understand the causes of risk, and how they work. A poor sense of danger results in driving at high risk without realising it - or being over-cautious.
- **Driving Experience:** is the store of your learning from previous driving - whenever you sat behind the wheel. This is where you keep most of your driving ability. Your experience <u>should</u> help you to make better judgements and decisions.

Notice that all your Knowledge and Beliefs exist even when you are not driving.

Fitness Check

Whether or not someone should drive is a simple, but critical, decision. And it involves three things:

- driver fitness — drink, drugs, tiredness, eyesight, emotional state, etc
- vehicle condition — steering, tyres, brakes, lights, etc
- road conditions — storm, blizzard, ice, fog, etc.

You assess each of these for risk as input to your Fitness Check decisions.

And getting it wrong will simply stack higher risk against you.

(The Risk Assessment step is described in detail below in the Control Cycle).

Although it is easy to recognise making this decision at the start of a journey, confirming it along the way is just as necessary. You may, for example, decide to stop if you become too tired, suspect a mechanical fault, or run into extreme weather.

The most common failure, of course, is in how
drivers assess their <u>own</u> fitness to drive!

Observation Cycle

Most danger on the road begins because someone fails to notice something important. And in general, drivers have poor observation. They miss a lot of detail in what is going on, and are easily distracted. But poor observation is often not as obvious as other errors that are made, and in this sense we could call it the "secret error".

The purpose of observation is to:

**collect the information needed to make the
right decisions about what to do.**

And it must search for <u>potential</u> dangers as well as tracking those that are already obvious.

Observation is the fastest spinning part of the driving process, with millisecond cycles that are often barely perceptible. For example, seeing brake lights ahead, anticipating the need to react, and deciding to glance behind - all happens in an instant.

It is a cycle in a continuous loop:

- **Observation Input:** is the information you gather from the driving situation. Which should include taking keen note of the results of your own actions.

- **Risk Assessment:** is where you understand the meaning of the input, and assess the danger.

- **Directing Attention:** uses your assessment of danger to decide where you will place your attention. It includes <u>when</u> you give attention to something, and for <u>how long</u>.

Risk Assessment

Observation Input
- find out what's happening
  - from all senses
- effects of actions taken

Directing Attention
- make decisions
  - where to look
  - use other senses

Driving Situation

Note that using your mirrors is in this step too - as part of "where to look".

Also decided is whether to accept distractions, such as adjusting the radio or heating, talking to passengers, etc. And in all of this, although observation is mainly about vision, your other senses are crucial too, such as hearing what is around, and feeling the motion of the car.

Control Cycle

The next step is to act on what you have observed. So the purpose is to decide what you are going to do, and to carry out the actions required. Whenever you choose to do the wrong thing, this is where it actually happens.

Also in this step is where your planning and thinking ahead takes place, which gains you extra time in deciding what to do. Essentially:

**this is where you exercise real control over the situations
you drive yourself into.**

This is another fast-moving cycle, with three steps:

- **Risk Assessment:** identifies all real and potential threats, and gauges how dangerous they are. This is where you understand your situation, and project it forward to anticipate what will, or could, happen next.

Good risk assessment picks up signs of danger very early.

It uses knowledge and reasoning about how and why events develop as they do.

Risk Assessment	Risk Control
- understand the situation - anticipate events - identify potential hazards - assess degree of danger	- make decisions - what actions to take - maintain a driving plan - intentions and options

Car Control
- steering   - clutch/gears - accelerator - indicators - brake   - lights

- **Risk Control:** contains your decisions about what to do, including the speed, direction and position that you want for the car.

It also decides what you <u>expect</u> to do next, and the alternatives you have if things change. This is your driving plan of "intentions and options", which is constantly rolling forward in front of you.

Driving Situation

- **Car Control:** is your execution of your decisions with the actions that make the car do what you want it to. This is where you use the car's controls:
    - mainly the ones that govern where the car goes - steering, accelerator, brake, clutch/gears
    - and others, such as: indicators, lights, horn, etc.

Learning From Experience

Most of any driver's skill is gained through the "experience" channel - learnt from actual driving. Reading a book, of course, helps by pointing the way!

How well this learning from experience works has a profound effect on the level of competence that is reached, and how quickly. And the crucial "purpose" of experience is:

**to harvest a steadily increasing skill
from your practical driving.**

This step looks deceptively simple, but things to note are that:
- the input is very broad. It includes everything you observe, the risks you sense, the decisions you make, and the outcome of your actions - all are available to build experience
- it works by finding reliable patterns in events that you can recognise in future situations to help you deal with them more quickly and safely
- it should also build an awareness of your own limitations, based on how you have been able to handle situations in the past.

Driving Experience

1.2.2 Putting it together

> <u>Key points</u>:   - **The full picture shows a new way to understand driving.**
>
>   - **And confirms how vital it is to actively manage risk.**

Having described each jigsaw piece separately, we can now put them together.

But the key is to first set the structure to fit them on to - just as an artist would paint his background before placing the subjects on to the canvas.

Our background here has four areas:

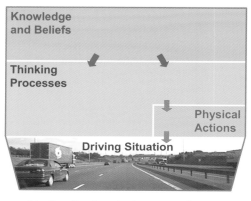

- **Knowledge and Beliefs:** for the elements of your memory.

- **Thinking Processes:** for making your decisions about what to do.

- **Physical Actions:** for carrying out what you decided to do.

- **Driving Situation:** for the total scene you are travelling in - which is ever changing and always unique to you. It is everything that could affect you, including what you don't know about. And as you respond to the situation, it also responds to you.

It includes:

- <u>all the road users</u>: drivers, cyclists, pedestrians, etc. What they are doing - and what they are thinking too!
- <u>all around you</u>: the roads, roadsides, footpaths, bridges, etc
- <u>the conditions</u>: weather, road surface, visibility, etc
- <u>your own vehicle</u>: its position, direction and speed, and its capability and condition. Also any passengers and load on board
- <u>yourself as the driver</u>: your skills, intentions and frame of mind.

Already, even in this background, a picture has started to take shape. Notice that there is:

- a clear distinction between **Knowledge and Beliefs** and **Thinking Processes**. This separation is important in untangling the mental activity
- a breadth in the **Driving Situation**, to include yourself, and things you don't know about. Every situation is unique in its detail, and never precisely repeated
- a simple chain-reaction that links down through the picture, as your **Knowledge and Beliefs** guide the **Thinking Processes** that decide the **Physical Actions** you take to move around in the **Driving Situation**.

And now finally, the five pieces can be put in place to reveal the whole picture. As you scan the diagram, you will recognise everything we discussed above. It is quite a full picture, because the task is a complex one.

These are the components of driving, and how they fit together!

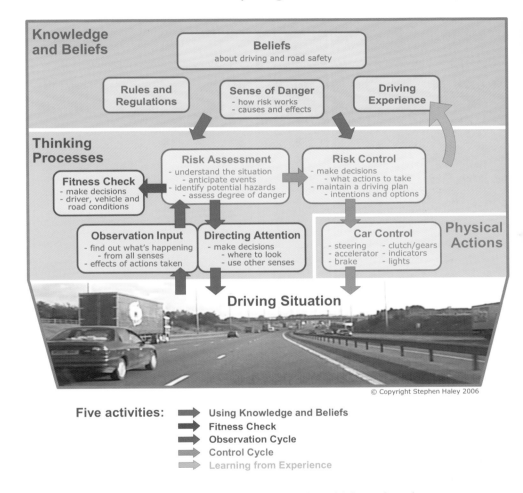

© Copyright Stephen Haley 2006

Five activities:
→ Using Knowledge and Beliefs
→ Fitness Check
→ Observation Cycle
→ Control Cycle
→ Learning from Experience

Take a while to digest it all. It is a striking new view of the driving task, and a cornerstone of the unique approach in this book.

Do not try to learn it, though! But do refer back to it as you go further into the book. And don't forget:

it is all working constantly, at the same time.

Other significant points are also highlighted:

- **Knowledge and Beliefs**
  - operates as a whole, and influences <u>all</u> of the thinking, not just some parts of it.

- **Observation Input**
  - is the <u>only</u> input you have from the **Driving Situation**. All your awareness comes in through this single channel.

- **Risk Assessment**
  - plays a vitally central role - taking part in all of the thinking processes.

- **Car Control**
  - contains all the actions you take to operate the car.

- **Learning from Experience**
  - comes from all of your thinking, not from any specific point.

Before leaving this stage, though, we should check something that was said at the start - that driving is an exercise in active risk management. So we should find that this is at the core of the picture. In business and in science, the methods for risk management have the same basic steps: monitor the situation, identify the hazards, quantify the risks, consider the options and decide on actions.

Checking the **Observation Cycle** and **Control Cycle** confirms that all the steps are there. These two cycles are at the very heart of the driving task, and they:

**capture what should always be running
in the front of your mind.**

1.2.3 Decisions, decisions...

<u>Key points</u>: - **Safety comes from the decisions you make.**

- **They are where you choose what you will try to do, and they determine the risks you will face.**

Very few people connect making decisions with driving, yet the Driving Process above mentions them a lot.

If you ask drivers, "What decisions do you make while driving?", most will struggle with the question. Eventually, the answer might be something like, "Where to go, and when to turn...?". The word "decision" seems strange in the context of driving.

And yet it is true that:

this is the most important thing we do.

The purpose of all your thinking skills is ultimately to make better decisions. And we define "better" to mean "safer". When we talk about managing risk - <u>this is how you do it</u>.

Whether or not they are aware of it, drivers are constantly deciding how fast, how close, when to go, when not to, and so on.

How well you handle the car itself plays a part too, but these decisions determine first what you will try to do.

However, it is:

reckless to assume that good decisions are just "common sense",

or are bestowed on drivers through rules and regulations. This is only the beginning of the expertise that you need.

In the driving process diagram there are three clear decision points:

1. **Fitness Check** - decides whether you drive at all, and whether you load the whole task with danger to begin with.

2. **Directing Attention** - determines what you find out about what is happening. This is the most constant and fastest-spinning set of decisions.

3. **Risk Control** - decides the actions you take, and the part you play in the total situation. This is how you commit your interaction with the road and other road users.

And decisions can be poor ones in many ways. They may be:

- wrong   - by increasing risk to a significant level
- slow   - events moved faster than the decision was made
- weak   - nervousness makes the action hesitant or incomplete
- absent   - a decision was needed but not taken - an "error of omission".

But to improve decisions we must first:

bring them to the surface.

And that is what this book does - even the subconscious ones. For some decisions this will be temporary, while they are worked on. A bit like taking an engine out on to the bench to overhaul it, and then returning it to the car. But you will find that others become a more permanent part of your conscious layer of thinking.

The nature of driving, though, puts:

particular pressures on decision-making that add to the difficulty.

And it is easy to list a number of these pressures:

- <u>rapid change</u> means that options must be constantly reconsidered
- the decisions are often <u>time-critical</u>, having to be taken at a precise moment
- there is always <u>uncertainty</u> in things you cannot know absolutely
- the <u>stakes are high</u>, with life-or-death decisions being required all the time
- all this generates a lot of <u>stress</u>... that only makes matters worse...

It might almost sound like an impossible task! But two very powerful techniques come to the rescue, and will help you to handle this wall of pressure:

1. Thinking Ahead

This means <u>expecting</u> to make the decisions, and:

> **preparing for the options in advance.**

It involves assessing a situation long before you arrive in it, and anticipating what might happen.

For example, a driver who comes to a busy roundabout without thinking must bring their lane to a halt while they start to look around. But, if they begin far back to see the traffic flows and assess the choices, the decision to enter is well planned. And when the moment comes, it can be made more quickly and safely for everyone.

2. Natural Intuition

This is how we <u>just know</u> what to do without having to think about everything as if for the first time. But do not confuse it with simply "guessing"! Take a trivial example. When you see: $15 - 5 = ?$, you just say 10. You don't count down from 15 on your fingers, or start wondering how to tackle the problem. You "know" the answer with absolute certainty.

It is a familiar query, with a natural response. In fact:

> **we use intuition all the time to solve most routine problems.**

Even as we walk around, this is what tells us how to avoid bumping into things. Intuition is built through learning from experience, and is a very effective and essential decision-making tool.

Experts, of course, can rely more on their intuition, because it is so good.

Significantly, these two techniques dispel the myth that fast decisions cannot be good ones. It is true, perhaps in business and government, that decisions are often based on working exhaustively through lists of pros and cons, and comparing various alternative courses of action to sift out the very best one.

But driving works at the opposite end of the scale, where time is short. So it is crucial to:

> **understand the difference between a "snap" decision and a "quick" one.**

The snap decision is an impulsive and hasty guess, but the quick one is expected and well prepared. Even so, quick decisions are not something to purposely "aim" for. Instead, they will come naturally as a consequence of improving your thinking skills in general.

It is also true that decision-makers who must work under time pressure take the first workable option they can find that meets the objective.

They act when it is "good enough", and then move on. For us, we can:

> **act on "negligible risk of collision",**

without spending more time trying to reduce risk further. Handling this constant compromise is a crucial part of the overall driving skill. And remember that searching for <u>zero</u> risk will prevent a workable decision - other than retiring to the armchair.

1.3 Skills and the Learning Curve

> **Key points:** - Gaining skill should start with a clear view of what there is to learn. You need to see the goal.
>
> - Otherwise the process is random and slow, and will harbour wasted potential.

Imagine a road network with no signs to show you where to go. The only places you could find would be the ones you already know, or others you just came across by chance.

It is a bit like that with driving ability.

After the initial training, we are:

  left to discover the most critical skills for ourselves

...by just driving around.

So it is essential to have a "roadmap" for the skills we want to gain.

In the last section, the elements of the driving task were drawn into a structured process diagram - and we can use it now to identify the skills. Following that, we will see how the skills can be plotted across stages of learning to give a very graphic picture of developing ability.

Driving is increasingly recognised as a life skill - alongside reading, numeracy, communicating, relationships, etc. It has become so essential in our way of life.

And this book uses:

  a deliberately broad definition of "skill".

If there is a right and a wrong way of doing something, and it is under our control, it is counted as a skill - because we can learn to do it better.

So this is definitely not restricted to the things we do with our hands and feet. It embraces all our <u>thinking</u> too, such as decisions about speed and whether we are too tired to drive. It also covers our <u>knowledge and beliefs</u>, so that knowing the Highway Code and having the right mindset are treated as skills as well.

1.3.1 Skills revealed

> <u>Key points</u>: - **There are eight specific skills in safe driving.**
>
> - **And they work together as an overall compound skill, in which they all play an essential part.**

Bringing all the abilities together into a single picture like this is much simpler to work with, and helps us think about them consistently. It captures in one sweep the full scope of the task - leaving nothing out. And it therefore:

> **brings together exactly what is under your control to be improved.**

Now let's get to the skills. Looking back at the process diagram, it becomes clear that by defining what we do:

> **we have <u>already</u> identified what we need to be good at.**

In other words, the skills can be immediately mapped directly on to the picture:

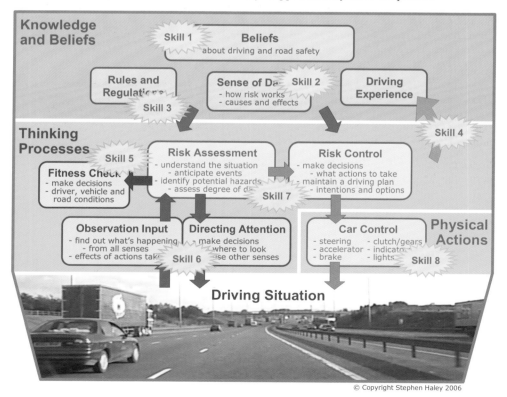

We find that eight skills cover the full task:

- **Knowledge and Beliefs**
  1. **Beliefs**
  2. **Sense of Danger**
  3. **Rules and Regulations**

- **Thinking Processes**
  4. Learning from Experience
  5. **Fitness Check**
  6. **Observation**
  7. **Risk Assessment and Control**

- **Physical Actions**
  8. **Car Control**

Again, take a while to digest the picture. Eight skills may be more than we expected - or even hoped for! But some critical new ones have emerged that were not very clear before.

Although we will discuss each skill separately, they should also be seen as a single "compound" ability. This means that the components must be combined together to be performed. Progress is then made in both sharpening the individual skills, and by:

integrating them together into a smooth flowing total skill.

So then, the overall standard is set by the weakest component, and our aim is to improve not just the parts that seem most obvious or easiest to do, but the skill in total. Indeed, an unbalanced ability can be actually dangerous. For example, if being brilliant at just **Car Control** leads you to believe you can handle any situation you meet.

As ability increases, the most critical skills become **Observation** and **Risk Assessment and Control**. In addition, the **Beliefs** and **Sense of Danger** also have an accelerating effect across other skills, because they help a lot of your thinking to fall into place. And Learning from Experience will be discussed later as the "crane that builds cranes" - the skill that builds all your other skills. The way these skills work so well together is what propels a rapid rise in ability.

So the emphasis in **Part 2: Gaining the skills** will be on these five skills, that really define the thinking part of driving:

- **Beliefs**
- **Sense of Danger**
- Learning from Experience
- **Observation**
- **Risk Assessment and Control**

These are also the ones that are harder for drivers to figure out well for themselves.

The other three skills are more traditional and already widely covered in the basic training and elsewhere:

- **Rules and Regulations**
- **Fitness Check**
- **Car Control**

They are more obvious in themselves too, and the coverage here can therefore be more brief.

1.3.2 The Learning Curve

Key points: - **Motivation to improve skill is stronger when it is clear what progress can be made.**

         - **Nearly all drivers can readily advance quickly far beyond their current level of ability.**

One of the most disturbing failures in road safety is the absence of a "learning culture" among motorists. Very few drivers see themselves as actively learning - they just drive.

When novices pass the test - with pride and great relief - their crisp new licence tells them they have legally learnt to drive! They never heard the examiner's caution about elementary skill, or perhaps even the mention of Pass Plus. The temptation is too great to race away with the notion that just "a bit more practice" will brush up any rough edges.

> But they have no idea, of course,
> how little skill they really have.

The old adage, "You really learn to drive after passing the test", makes very little sense to them, and the fantasy survives - that they have done what is necessary.

So then, turning their miles into ability is random and shapeless - a journey of "learning by accident". Progress is slow, and skill easily stagnates far short of its potential. This can persist through a whole driving career, with some of the crucial skills being barely learned at all. But fortunately, to change this for yourself is not difficult. And in fact, of course, you have already started!

Discarding the old pattern begins with making sure we have a very good picture of exactly what there is to learn.

And this essential first step was taken in the previous section by defining the eight specific skills.

Building on this, we can then give the learning process itself a much more tangible shape by seeing it as <u>five</u> distinct stages from Beginner to Expert.

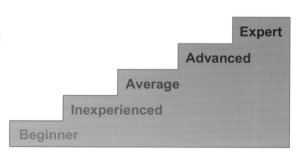

A similar approach has been used for skills outside the sphere of driving, and works very well.

We can describe these stages as:

Beginner	just starting out, focused totally on passing the test. On average, drives only about 600 miles in this stage.
Inexperienced	has passed the test, is suddenly driving alone, and mainly reacting to situations created by other people.
Average	has reached the level of skill that happens more or less by itself. This is the vast majority, the middle 80%.
Advanced	consciously taking skills to a higher level. The Advanced tests are in this stage, but not a prerequisite.
Expert	has become a master in all of the skills. The complete expert remains a point at the top of the curve for everyone to aim at.

And even further, the skills can then be plotted across these stages to build into a striking curve of rising overall expertise:

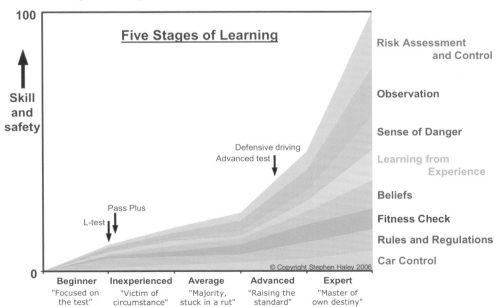

The skills that feature most in basic training have been put broadly towards the bottom of the stack, and the less taught ones are towards the top. This emphasises the process of building on the traditional base, and shows just how much the highly skilled driver has added to it.

Some key points are graphically illustrated:
- the huge safety opportunity that is seized by gaining skill
- exactly what is missing in the early stages of ability
- the stagnation of the majority in Average, with low learning
- the steep rise into Advanced and Expert, for anyone who decides to improve
- everyone has something to go for, and can feel motivated up the curve.

The shape of this picture has met with broad agreement across a wide range of drivers and instructors. But if you find yourself wanting to adjust it in some way, then it has started to work - you are <u>thinking</u> about it! Effectively, it represents a curve of "safety benefit", showing the purpose and reward of gaining skills. And throwing the picture into such sharp focus should fuel the desire to move up it.

Also important is a distinct transition that occurs across the chart. Rising from the early stages to the higher levels there is a strong change:

from a mainly "rule-guided" ability to a mainly "experience-guided" one.

In every field of human endeavour, high expertise is defined by developing very good, solid judgement, based on experience.

But there is a potential pitfall here too, since everyone is tempted to place themselves as far up the curve as they dare. Indeed, we all have moments of brilliance, and they are rightly prized. But over-estimating your ability can only backfire. What matters is what you do consistently - not just occasionally. So:

when assessing your own skill be realistic, even conservative.

There is a well known "delusion of competence" in which most drivers believe they have far higher than average skill. It is based on the flaws in subjective judgement. Techniques for more objective self-assessment are included later when we look at the skills in detail.

It is natural, though, that high skill in anything holds a certain mystery. Indeed, there is a "one way street" in our perception. You can imagine a lower skill than your own quite easily, because you recall being at that stage yourself. But:

a <u>higher</u> skill is more difficult to imagine.

So the talents of a snooker champion or premier league footballer may look like magic to the rest of us. And similarly in driving, an expert's quick and effortless decisions may look strange, or even rash, to a less able driver. Also, when depending crucially on others, as we do on the roads, we are especially uncomfortable to trust in an ability we don't understand. And this makes us reluctant to believe that others might be more skilled than we are.

Returning to the stages of skill, it can be useful to illustrate them with brief descriptions. The Institute of Advanced Motorists, for example, describe their members as: "confident and decisive, but never reckless... enthusiastic about driving and make better progress than most other drivers".

In a similar way, the next table shows the solid progress across the stages. You need not be at the same stage in them all at the same time, of course.

	Beginner Focused on the test	**Inexperienced** Victim of circumstance	**Average** Majority, stuck in a rut	**Advanced** Raising the standard	**Expert** Master of own destiny
Risk Assessment and Control	Very limited. No forward planning. Highly reactive. Decisions are often nervous and late. Frequent errors. Lacks judgement.	Exploring through mistakes. Reactive style, with little anticipation or judgement. Relies on others for safety without realising it.	Mediocre ability. Limited by lack of attention and low understanding of danger. Still unaware of many risks being taken.	In tune with events. Thinks ahead, and anticipates danger well, with good judgement in dealing with it.	In control of the situation. Proactive style, planning far ahead. Predicts almost everything that happens. Very rarely surprised. Reliable instincts and accurate judgements.
Observation	Very limited. Must be told what to watch for. Can miss obvious dangers. No sense of the total situation. Attention is tense.	Able to focus more of attention outside the car. But is easily overloaded and finds it hard to know what is important.	Has fallen into routines. Welcomes the opportunity to devote less attention to the task. Misses a lot of what is important.	Knows observation is critical. Maintains high concentration. Wide focus, with a good sense of what is relevant.	Deep perception of everything going on. Always super-alert. Notices fine detail, with an acute sense of what is relevant. High concentration is relaxed and effortless.
Sense of Danger	Only sees the obvious dangers. Every hazard is a separate event.	Beginning to see more dangers, and to connect events into a flow.	Recognises familiar dangers, but with limited grasp of underlying causes.	Increasing instincts for the causes of danger, but with little structure.	Comprehensive model of risk, covering all causes of danger, and a thorough grasp of how they behave.
Beliefs	Will "believe" whatever is needed to pass the test. Responsibility for actions is assigned to the rules being followed.	Suddenly alone, and testing different driving styles. Can easily become overconfident. Still assigns responsibility to the rules.	Behaviour is usually acceptable, though not always consistent or sensitive to the needs of others.	Very conscious of a high standard of conduct. But probably does not work to explicit beliefs.	Has a full set of explicit beliefs. Is consciously aware of how powerfully they influence decisions and behaviour.
Learning from Experience	Learning is tense. High attention is on practicing using the controls. Feedback from events is low.	Learning is more relaxed, but random. Beginning to see the limitations of basic training.	Skill is stagnated. Does not know how to learn any more. May respond badly to suggestions.	Strong desire to learn, but limited in knowing how to do so. Makes good but uneasy progress.	Knows how to monitor performance. Learning is integral to the task. It is methodical, highly effective and always working.
Fitness Check	On best behaviour for lessons. Relies on the car owner for vehicle safety, and on instructor to be sensitive to road conditions.	Thrilled to be mobile. May unknowingly take risks with personal fitness and road conditions. Detects only obvious mechanical faults.	Routinely stretches personal limits. Mechanical awareness is quite limited. Often optimistic about road conditions.	Never drives when unfit. Sensitive to mechanical problems when driving. Takes good account of road conditions.	Plans activities to ensure fit to drive when required. Highly sensitive to the car. Detects and attends to problems early. Avoids driving in unsuitable conditions.
Rules and Regulations	Studiously learned for the test. This is the main basis for safety at this level.	Increased understanding, but memory begins to fade. Still the main basis of safety.	Rule-following is strained, but with nothing to replace it. Some rules are easily forgotten.	Revision has restored memory. Sees the rules in a broader context.	Understands the rules, and has a deep sense of their underlying purpose and shortcomings.
Car Control	Movements are awkward and need a lot of attention. The car is an alien object.	Driving alone makes practice less self-conscious. More natural movements emerge.	Using controls has become automatic, though may include some unsafe habits.	Smooth operation of all controls, though may be rule-guided about when to use them.	Car is fully a natural extension of the body. Controls are applied with precision, and matched to the situation exactly. Focused on the result.

The two sides of the table give a stark comparison. The Beginners feel remote from what they are doing, with tense and exhausting concentration. They are overloaded by complexity, struggle to see what is important, and therefore think slowly and must clutch on to rules just to barely cope. This is the "hardest" way of driving.

In total contrast, the Experts feel deeply involved and relaxed, with a keen and effortless attention. They have a profound grasp of the task which makes it simple, so that excellent decisions are made quickly and easily by knowing intuitively what to do. This is much easier on the human frame.

The essential truth is that nearly all drivers can readily achieve a far higher level of skill than they currently have. Once it has been demystified.

Next, in **Part 2: Gaining the skills**, we step through each skill in detail.

Part 2: Gaining the skills

Key points: - Gaining ability will take time, and involves exercising the new skills out on the road.

- As you build the set of eight skills, your overall level of competence is governed by the weakest link.

Now to the real meat of the matter - how to gain the skills. As you would expect, this is the major part of the book.

To get the most from this section, you should first have read **Part 1: Defining the skills**. It gives a new structure to the task of driving, and explains not only what the skills are, but also why. With this firm grasp, it is easier to:

set about learning the right things,

that will be effective in what you are trying to do.

Recall from before, that safe driving is a mainly thinking task. And this thinking is about active risk management, and how you reach your decisions about what to make the car do.

In the last chapter a deliberately broad definition of "skill" was taken, to build a complete picture. And this gave us eight skills:

- **Knowledge and Beliefs**
  1. Beliefs
  2. Sense of Danger
  3. Rules and Regulations

- **Thinking Processes**
  4. Learning from Experience
  5. Fitness Check
  6. Observation
  7. Risk Assessment and Control

- **Physical Actions**
  8. Car Control

These were also mapped on to a five-stage learning curve of overall safe skill.

Of these skills, **Observation** and **Risk Assessment and Control** have by far the biggest coverage in the following pages. At the expert level, they have the highest ultimate contribution to safety. Firmly underpinning these are **Beliefs**, **Sense of Danger** and Learning from Experience. Taken together, these five skills are:

the core of your "eyes and brain" ability.

The more traditional skills in **Rules and Regulations**, **Fitness Check** and **Car Control** are outlined more briefly because these three are already extensively covered in basic training. Some important points are still made, though.

Recall too, that all eight skills are components of the single "compound skill" of safe driving.

Because of this:

**one weak link can badly limit
your overall ability.**

So this section examines each skill in turn, and how to improve it. But remember that reading a book can only do so much.

Gaining genuine skill and reaping the reward lies in what you <u>do</u>. And the true aim is in the practice and exercise of the skills out on the road.

With all of the information and techniques, though, apply them progressively, rather than impatiently. Expect that absorbing a fresh skill to the point where it becomes instinctive will take time. And don't suddenly throw your attention on to something new to the exclusion of all else.

Let the base of skills build steadily and solidly - at its own pace.

Also don't forget, that if you are waiting for where this book gives you specific instructions to follow in all the various driving situations, stop looking. It does not do that. Instead, the aim is to equip you with the thinking to <u>make your own good decisions</u>, and take control of your own safety. This is much more effective, and some would say is an overdue departure from the traditional approach.

In truth, it increasingly becomes a freedom to enjoy!

Skill 1: Beliefs

> <u>Key point</u>:   - Everything you do is guided by your basic beliefs,
> and controlling danger is much easier with the
> right ones.

Imagine that what you do is subject to just two types of control - external and internal.

External controls are the rules that come from someone else. And internal control is exercised from your own beliefs about what is right.

Ideally, they should match quite well - or your life will be full of conflicts. Of the two, though, your internal beliefs are the deeper influence. They are the values you live by. They shape your reasoning and judgement, and govern your "voluntary" actions.

Your beliefs about driving are, therefore, vital

and act as a directing hand over everything you think and do on the road. And they cannot be "faked" either, because the acid test is in what you actually do. Whatever you <u>say</u> you believe, or think you <u>should</u> believe do not count at all.

Crucially too:

no one else can <u>tell</u> you what to believe.

Trying to do so just triggers resistance.

Someone may successfully tell you what to <u>do</u>, but not what to believe. The best they can do is advise, explain and lead by example.

Has someone ever told you to "Change your attitude!"? How did you react...?

But your beliefs are also much broader and deeper than just attitude. And deciding on what they will be is even more something that you do for yourself.

This contrasts strongly with the "rules" of the road, which <u>are</u> put in place by external instruction, and rightly so. They include the motoring laws, traffic signs and rules in the Highway Code.

So this chapter offers a "mindset" that will help you to control risk. It is expressed as a set of simple personal beliefs - as if you were saying them yourself. The more of them you are able to genuinely adopt, the safer you will be, and as we said:

this is your own decision.

If there are any that you hesitate over, try asking yourself if you would like other road users to have the belief, and see if it helps to convince you.

Putting these beliefs together in a set, and stating them explicitly, is a very powerful base for your skills. And remember that whatever mindset you choose to have, it definitely <u>will</u> guide every thought you have and every action you take.

2.1.1 Safety

What is important in a journey? Modern motoring is usually a very functional task of just getting from A to B, but we probably have a list of other objectives in mind too, such as:

- travelling in comfort
- getting there quickly
- avoiding stress
- enjoying the journey
- arriving safely
- practising and improving driving skills
- avoiding boredom
- etc...

But you may be confused by the sequence of this list - if you expected it to be in some sort of order. It is purposely jumbled. In truth, everyone will have their own priorities. Yet every day you will meet drivers who seem to be getting them wrong, and it helps to give your own objectives some thought.

Although your list may change from day to day, or even during a journey:

there is one aim that should always be at the top.

And it will help you to position the others. It is simply <u>to arrive safely</u>.

Because there is little point in setting out without this as the most important thing, it should be easy to accept. No objective in a journey is more vital, and this becomes, therefore, your own simple pre-condition for everything you do.

> <u>Belief 1:</u> **Arriving safely is the most important thing - for me and for everyone else.**

2.1.2 Thinking, risk and decisions

Each of these three topics have been discussed earlier. But taken together they form a basic belief that will:

help you to focus on the right things.

The main points are:

- safety always begins in your <u>thinking</u>. This puts the right perspective on the role played by the "eyes and brain" skills in your head, versus the ones in your hands and feet

- the thinking is about <u>risk management</u>, which is a balancing task using specific skills. Don't forget that safety can only be pursued through the active control of risk. You cannot directly inject "safety" into your driving. It would be like trying to pour "emptiness" into a glass to get the contents out

- risk is controlled through the <u>decisions</u> you make (or don't make). These will determine when and how you expose yourself to danger.

> <u>Belief 2</u>: **Safe driving is in my thinking. It is about actively managing risk with the decisions I make.**

2.1.3 Blame

No one wants to be blamed for things that go wrong. It is a bad feeling. So deep in human nature:

we have a reluctance to accept blame.

And some trends in our society not only allow this, but even seem to encourage it. There is rising concern over the compensation culture of "blame-and-claim", in which people try diligently to blame someone else for the misfortunes that befall them. Law firms advertise with enticing slogans, such as: "Where there's blame, there's a claim", and "No win, no fee". These appeal to the need to be innocent, and to greed at the same time - a very powerful duo. Claims in the courts have spiralled with the inflamed enthusiasm for being cast as a victim. There are many worthy cases, of course, but as a culture it holds a damaging attitude.

In driving, "Not my fault..." is a particularly reckless frame of mind - and futile too. An epitaph of "Innocent Victim" chiselled tenderly in polished granite is by that stage a very empty virtue. Surviving is more important than being "right"!

Even more crucially, being preoccupied with who is to blame will:

lead you to ignore dangers that you could easily resolve.

And to practise a selfish refusal to help others when they need it is self-defeating for your own safety as well.

Don't be confused, either, by the interest that insurers and the police must take in who was at fault. This is <u>after</u> the event of a crash. Up to that point, the vital thing is to <u>avoid the crash</u>. Allocating blame only makes sense when <u>everyone's</u> efforts to control the danger have failed.

> **Belief 3:** **Preventing a collision is more important than who would be to blame for it.**

2.1.4 Responsibility

Being reminded that using the roads is a privilege, not a right, is often hard to accept. Such is the importance of mobility in our lives. But:

> **the fact that you can put other people in danger makes sense of it.**

And responsibility is the key to earning the privilege.

However, the culture of shedding blame seen above also weakens people's willingness to take responsibility for their actions, and to look after themselves. And this, in turn, makes life more dangerous for everyone.

In driving, safety is increased by accepting two obligations:

1. <u>responsibility for your own actions</u> (or lack of them):
   - this is an absolute. You cannot deny responsibility for any of your own actions
   - you should also never rely on someone else to make safe a risk that you created, such as "He should have braked - he saw me turning out!"
   - neither can you blame someone else for enticing you into doing something reckless.

2. <u>responsibility for protecting yourself</u> against danger created by others:
   - at first this may seem an unbalanced burden to take on. But why would you put yourself at the mercy of someone else's carelessness? So it is basic self-preservation, and the strongest interest in that is your own
   - it is also true that nearly all crashes could have been prevented by <u>any</u> of the parties involved. So coping practically with other people's errors is vital to your own safety. Clearly, this has failed if someone hits you
   - lastly, if you don't actively protect yourself you are more likely to demand that everyone else is a perfect road user - which leads to a very aggressive and unrealistic style.

The best drivers treat their situation as their own creation - even though there are others involved too. In almost every crash, there is something you could have done to prevent it.

> **Belief 4:** **I take responsibility for my total situation - everything I do, and protecting myself from others.**

2.1.5 Skills and learning

Skills

Driving uses many skills. And <u>safe</u> driving needs even more. As we saw before, some of the skills are well understood, and others are not. But they are all vital parts in a total skill, that is only as strong as its weakest point. Typically, for instance, superb car handling and lightning reactions may be useful in some situations, but can be treacherous if exploited in isolation. In contrast, a more balanced high level of skill will earn extreme safety.

However, there are some common complacencies about skills - including that they can be:
- gained from just browsing a book in an armchair
- neglected without losing their edge
- over-estimated without consequence.

These are all false, of course, because:

expertise is built and maintained through solid practice.

In fact, your "available skills" are the ones you routinely use and keep sharp. There is little value in being a "potentially" expert driver. Therefore, your skills <u>are</u> the way you drive.

Alongside that, though, being highly skilled should not make you feel superior or overconfident. That would plunge you headlong into one of the most obvious traps. The aim is to benefit from your skill, not to feel compelled to prove it, or test it to destruction.

Learning

How many qualified drivers would describe themselves as learners? We could guess it would be very few. "Learners" want to quickly leave that stage behind. Yet passing the test should not mark the end of learning, but the start of an even more vital phase altogether.

In practice, people who are expert at something are far more likely to see themselves as constant learners. Quite unsurprisingly:

that is how they became so good!

And in the same way, you should think of yourself as always learning on the road. Indeed, we can readily admit that everyone makes mistakes, and that every error holds a lesson.

Being open to learning rests on this blunt honesty that there is always something to work on. Without it, your learning will happen just by chance, or might even be resisted. Clearly, any ability only becomes a "life skill" through lifelong learning.

You can also learn from things that go well, of course. And this is much more enjoyable, even though the events may be less evident at first because they are not threatening. Nevertheless, they are just as valuable.

Even so, learning on your own can be difficult. But just deciding to do it gets past the first major hurdle, and paves the way to learning naturally as a matter of routine.

> <u>Belief 5</u>:   **I control risk by gaining and using the right skills, and driving within my ability. I am constantly learning.**

2.1.6 Concentration, distraction and emotion

Concentration

Whatever skill you have, it is brought to bear in just one way - through concentration.

Focusing your attention is the channel for all your ability. Indeed, concentration has been called the supreme ability in itself, because achieving anything involves first applying your mind to it.

But this does not mean <u>forced</u> concentration. Demanding the brain to concentrate is too tiring, especially for a long time. The effort turns into a stressful blockage as the task becomes the "trying" to concentrate. So it is wrong to think of concentration as staring rigidly at something with a tense frown, or even thinking hard about it. Instead:

your attention is best when it is <u>attracted</u> to a task.

When something captures your interest by itself, a relaxed spiral is started. As you want to apply yourself... you do a better job... enjoy it more... feel more involved... and so on. This is <u>natural</u> concentration, that builds on itself. It is voluntary, spontaneous and without tension - the total opposite of forced concentration.

Experts in diverse fields, from musicians to fighter pilots, will talk of a Zen-like state of "effortless effort", when their mind has calmly locked on to what it is doing. Being "at one" with the task is then deeply rewarding in itself. Sporting champions also call this being "in the zone".

In driving, the trigger for natural concentration is easy to find. It starts the moment you show an interest in what safer driving is, and how to do it. As you then investigate and make more sense of it, you will gain more control, and feel a closer connection to the task.

This self-rewarding spiral is exactly how learning is accelerated naturally, along with a heightened enjoyment too, which is also important.

Distraction

A distraction is anything that takes your attention off where it should be. The exact opposite of concentration.

And they come in many forms - in your thoughts, or something to look at, or something that occupies your hands. Or perhaps all three at once, such as when dialling or sending a text on a mobile phone!

But it is impossible to legislate distractions out of driving - or anything else. The mind will always seek out something it finds fascinating. And driving can be a boring chore for anyone who has not discovered something appealing in it. Indeed:

the "normal" level of attention for average drivers runs at around 20%,

which explains a lot just by itself.

Part of the problem is undoubtedly the deceptive simplicity of a car's controls, that allows a feeling that not much attention is needed. But the lure of distractions then takes hold. So deciding where <u>not</u> to put your attention is as vital as deciding where it <u>should</u> be.

Emotion

Emotions are powerful things, and profoundly effect how you react to the world around you. They can be strong distractions, that interfere with your judgement too.

As you drive, many emotions can be at work, either as part of what you are doing or from something else. Such as:

- frustration/anger   - makes you aggressive, and even want to "hurt" someone
- nervousness/fear   - makes you over-cautious, with weak decisions and late actions
- ego/status/envy   - makes you want to prove superiority or defend territory
- worry/sorrow/grief   - takes your thoughts elsewhere, miles away from your driving.

Of course, to have feelings is unavoidable, even when driving. For example, man is a territorial animal by nature, and the car is a piece of mobile territory. So this makes us quite prone to act in territorial defence. And frustration, which is increasing on the roads, is a strong aggravating factor. There is also more congestion, tighter schedules to meet, and life in general is more stressed. Unfortunately, though, evolution has designed us very badly to be so compressed against strangers, and against time. And then through all of this, we do more and more driving!

Probably the most dangerous emotion in driving is anger. We all feel it, and will sometimes find it hard to control. But when it spirals into threatening behaviour, it becomes the all too familiar "road-rage". In Australia they call this "predatory driving", to describe even better its targeted nature. "Red mist" is also a term used for the state of mind when judgement has been overtaken by rage.

However, most important is not whether you <u>feel</u> emotions - it is how you <u>deal</u> with them. And:

the key is to simply
separate your emotions from your actions.

For example, <u>feeling</u> angry can be separated from <u>driving</u> angry. Achieving such a separation gets easier with practice, but starts with the simple intention to do so.

For most emotions, especially the ones above, the best state of mind for driving is to be "emotionally neutral". This gives you the clear and level head that you need for high concentration and objective judgement. Any decisions you make that are charged with emotion will not be the best you can do.

<u>Belief 6</u>: **My skills are best applied through natural concentration. I knowingly resist distractions, and try to keep emotions in neutral.**

2.1.7 Aggression

Linked to emotions is aggression, which is worthy of a "belief" all of its own. It is the area that is most usually referred to as "attitude".

The causes of aggressive driving vary widely. It may happen in a brief and isolated moment, or can be part of a more permanent style. A specific event may trigger a short spark of anger or frustration, for example. But an aggressive <u>style</u> is likely to come from a more deep-seated insecurity and a need to show dominance that is rooted elsewhere in the driver's life.

If anyone is unaware of crossing into this territory, unsure of where the boundary is:

aggression has an unmistakable character
that totally gives the game away.

It has a razor-sharp definition that sets it apart from any other style. You have passed into aggression when:

1. <u>safety is no longer the top priority</u> - some other personal triumph has become more important. Interactions with others are used as power struggles, with cooperation seen as a weakness, and dangers are deliberately left for someone else to handle

2. <u>there is a willingness to create risk</u> - instead of trying to reduce it. And:

the aggression is clearly used to <u>intimidate</u> people.

This very obviously describes an offensive (rather than defensive) style, and a form of "perpetual novice", who is trapped in poor skill.

Be aware, though, that "aggressive" is not the same as "assertive". We should use "assertive" to mean a positive style that not only still has safety as the top priority, but also <u>actively reduces</u> danger.

In your mind, you probably link aggression with someone who forces impatiently through traffic, or wants to go unreasonably fast. But there are other common aggressive behaviours too, such as:

- the "slow aggressive", who insists that, "Everyone else will just have to wait!", without caring how much congestion, frustration and danger is caused around them
- the "rolling obstructer" who blocks the road, such as the middle or outside lane of a motorway, to deliberately stop others going past
- the "civilian enforcer" who uses his vehicle to stop other people doing anything he believes is wrong. Again, this often means preventing others from passing.

Whatever its source or flavour, aggression will always increase risk. And <u>self</u>-control is at least as important as car control.

> **Belief 7:** I keep aggression out of my driving. It always increases risk.

2.1.8 Tolerance, cooperation and courtesy

When we drive, it is usually among total strangers. Yet the activity of "interacting journeys" clearly works best as a team effort, where the aim is to get everyone "home" safely to their destination. The team is everyone around you. So it is ever-changing, yet also always the same - a collection of strangers.

But there is no opposing team to compete against. Instead, the adversary is the intrusion of risk into what you are all doing. Like conquering a mountain together, ultimately you all share a single common goal. So the best performance comes from being unified in the task, and:

placing the collective good above personal gain.

Sound tough? This is what all top teams do.

As is normal, your "team members" will have different levels of skill, and you should accept that. Some will be very capable, and others will need a lot of help. Some may struggle to contribute usefully at all. But your total well-being still rests on how you treat each other - mainly in the three ways below.

Tolerance

All the time, you will meet road users who make mistakes - mainly small ones. Probably you normally think that they really should know better. But don't overlook that intolerance is a type of hypocrisy, because you make mistakes too. And, as we said before, to insist that everyone else is perfect is a very aggressive demand.

So the supreme response to errors is always the same - to <u>forgive</u>. And help to keep the danger small. Sometimes it might be hard not to react differently, especially if you felt threatened and that pumped a little adrenalin. But reacting offensively invites the inflamed spiral into road-rage as we saw before. It is important to realise that:

mistakes are rarely either
deliberate or aimed at you personally.

And offering tolerance is also a far more pointed lesson to the error-maker than insisting on a bout of gladiatorial combat.

Even more importantly, tolerance is essential if you want to predict other people's errors calmly, and allow for them safely. You should, of course, still hold strong views on driving standards, but not wield them as a weapon.

Cooperation

In addition to reacting well to errors, road users can do much more for each other.

While making progress along your own journey, you can consciously "allow and assist" everyone else in their journey too. This means helping rather than obstructing them, and:

not competing for space or position on the road.

Maximising the overall flow will eventually be in your own interest too.

Certainly, our society thrives on competition, which it sees as healthy. Stronger, higher, quicker - beating someone else can be highly respected and rewarded. But on the road it works in reverse. The battling ego must stay in the box, as the challenge is switched towards the team effort against the elements, not against each other.

The spirit of cooperation is a very safe one - even if, as they might, some people just take advantage of it.

Courtesy

Closely linked to cooperation is your wider consideration for others. This is also powerful in reducing risk by keeping everyone calm - and happy to cooperate.

It must be used sensibly, though, and:
> **there should always be a clear net gain across the total situation.**

It is not valid, for example, to bring a 40mph line of steady traffic to an abrupt halt to let a friend out of a side road. The harm would far outweigh the good as a surge of heavy braking swept back along the line. The decision would have sacrificed the safe and smooth flow, and the wake of "discourtesy" rippling out from the action would be too big.

Especially important is that other road users see the action as reasonable, and no one is surprised by it. An inappropriate courtesy will generate danger. But used properly, courtesy is one of the best ways to encourage cooperation.

> <u>Belief 8:</u> **Safe driving is a team effort. I forgive mistakes made by others, will help where I can, and offer courtesy where it is safe and practical.**

2.1.9 Influence

One of the most infectious things for the human race is the way we behave. Even in adults, imitation is a most natural learning process.

So everyone is impressionable, and will tend to mimic what happens around them. In crowds, we see people getting "caught up" in what is going on - often to do quite uncharacteristic things. At some level, we are each keen to fit in, which means we can quite quickly and subconsciously absorb the norms and values from our surroundings.

We are all role models for each other. And we are especially sensitive to behaviour we directly receive - the things that are "done" to us. Unfortunately though, the wrong behaviour is often most readily copied, and a good influence may be hard to find.

This is how life is often a reflection... Without thinking about it, you will naturally play your part in reflecting back to others the way that they treat you. If someone is pleasant and amenable to you, you are unlikely to pick an argument with them. And if they are aggressive you are unlikely to want to feel pleasant and amenable in return.

On the road, the point is that you should:

be careful what influences you allow yourself to pick up.

In addition to bad influence presenting itself more prominently, you might also be in a territorial frame of mind too. And the consequences are potentially far more dire than a little social friction.

So it is worth deliberately guarding against influences you don't want to absorb.

And what should you do about your outward influence on others? Well, just think what sort of driving you want reflected back at you. This makes it very simple. Any form of aggression or obstruction should definitely be out. And instead should come the tolerance, cooperation and courtesy that we saw the value of before - the "common goal" approach.

Belief 9:   **From all the behaviour displayed on the road, I take only the best as an example to follow.**

2.1.10 Pride and pleasure

Allowing yourself to feel good is vital in anything you want to do well. It is hard to give your best to something you would rather not be doing. And driving is also probably:

too much a part of your life to accept it as just a tedious chore.

In truth, though, the number of us who actively enjoy driving has been falling for some time, from one in two in 1991 to one in four in 2004. This is an unhelpful trend that is worth reversing - if only for yourself.

Definitely, it is okay to take pride in doing something well - in fact, more than okay. Being proud of your skills is one of the well deserved rewards for having them. It helps you to value them, and makes your learning even more enjoyable. Without, of course, getting overblown into conceit or arrogance! Let's just feel good about being good at something.

Let's also break the irrational taboo that some people would put around fun. Enjoyment is not another word for recklessness. Put aside the implication from the criminal act of "joy-riding". We can have fun without being dangerous. Indeed, the expert control of risk is a far better buzz than anything about losing it, because:

the highest thrill is in mastering what we do.

Being too serious is also a definite drain on enthusiasm. Motoring should not be just grim and dull, with a pressured monotony. You should take pleasure in the freedom, and what it helps you to do. Feeling such enjoyment will surely lift your performance.

Belief 10:   **I take pride in my skills, and enjoy driving! This helps to keep me naturally focused on the task.**

2.1.11 Summary beliefs

Now we can summarise the beliefs for easy reference. Some of them may still give a bit of a jolt, being expressed so bluntly. And you may want time to reflect on them a while.

But if you are uncertain about accepting any of them, ask whether your doubts are likely to increase or decrease the danger that you get yourself into. Also, as we said at the start, ask yourself if you would like other people to have the belief.

1.	Safety	Arriving safely is the most important thing - for me and for everyone else.
2.	Thinking, Risk and Decisions	Safe driving is in my thinking. It is about actively managing risk with the decisions I make.
3.	Blame	Preventing a collision is more important than who would be to blame for it.
4.	Responsibility	I take responsibility for my total situation - everything I do, and protecting myself from others.
5.	Skills and Learning	I control risk by gaining and using the right skills, and driving within my ability. I am constantly learning .
6.	Concentration, Distraction and Emotion	My skills are best applied through natural concentration. I knowingly resist distractions, and try to keep emotions in neutral.
7.	Aggression	I keep aggression out of my driving. It always increases risk.
8.	Tolerance, Cooperation and Courtesy	Safe driving is a team effort. I forgive mistakes made by others, will help where I can, and offer courtesy where it is safe and practical.
9.	Influence	From all the behaviour displayed on the road, I take only the best as an example to follow.
10.	Pride and Pleasure	I take pride in my skills, and enjoy driving! This helps to keep me naturally focused on the task.

Declaring your beliefs to yourself is a crucial step - in anything you do. In driving, they are your foundation for building safety. It is like setting conscious aims that spur you on towards what you want to achieve.

Always remember that the beliefs you choose to hold <u>will</u> shape your thinking, and guide everything you do.

Skill 2: Sense of danger

Key points: - **Without a good sense of danger you cannot be safe.**

                          - **Most motorists have a poor sense of where danger really comes from.**

Unless you know what danger is, you can't control it. This is an obvious statement - but it uncovers a big problem, because:

most people are wildly overconfident about their understanding of where danger comes from.

If you ask any bunch of people, "What are the causes of danger on the road?", everyone's list will be different.

And they would include a lot of things they just wish other people would not do. But these are things you can't control, which is not very useful.

So this chapter looks at the causes of danger that are in every situation, and in a way that you <u>can</u> control. It will give you:

a grasp of danger that enables you to successfully manage risk.

This is the core of how the whole new approach to safe driving began.

However, there are two ideas that allow people to put off thinking much about danger.

Firstly, the highways are, fortunately, quite forgiving places. Most mistakes have little consequence, so we get away with them. And this regular support from good fortune lets us ignore the errors. After all, why would you dwell on things that don't seem to matter?

But if it takes a crash or near miss to catch your attention, then experience is a very bad teacher. It invites you to continue to gamble on the leniency of fate.

It also confuses your sense of danger since most of it is shrugged off.

So a pattern emerges where minor errors are repeated, and grow into bigger ones - until disaster strikes and inflicts a severe punishment.

Secondly, and even more of a hindrance, is that we deliberately blame bad luck for crashes.

> We call them "accidents". Which is a wonderfully convenient word, meaning "an event without apparent cause, a happening by chance".
>
> What a superb release from feeling responsible!

With these two millstones around the collective mind of motorists, it is not surprising that a lot of danger is ignored, and:

> **the average sense of danger is quite poorly developed.**

Specifically frail are the abilities to:

- detect risks very early, when they are easier to handle
- assess danger objectively, when luck can so often seem to affect the outcome
- control threats actively to keep them at a safe level.

The following sections examine the causes of risk quite radically, and build into a simple model that will:

- explain risk in terms you can detect and make decisions about
- show how danger always has multiple causes
- give a clear structure for a vast expansion in your thinking about danger.

2.2.1 Defining risk

> **Key point:**   - **Risk is about the <u>probability</u> and the <u>consequences</u> of a collision. And they should not be confused.**

We said before that risk is inevitable in driving. And that in practical terms, "safe" must actually be a deliberate reduction of danger, by actively managing risk. Furthermore, it is pointless to demand that risk is zero, or that someone else should take care of it.

The start point is:

> **to be totally clear about what risk really is.**

Turning again to the dictionary, the definition of "risk" refers to the chance of something happening, and the bad consequences.

This is immediately useful in separating two things that are often confused:

1. the <u>probability</u> of a collision happening
2. the <u>consequences</u> if it does.

The first is about avoiding a crash, and the second is about how severe it would be.

For example, if you suddenly meet a tight bend on a wet night there is a certain chance that you might skid off the road. But if the edge is a flat grass verge the scenario is different to it being a sheer mountain drop. Your problem is rather different in each case - and your thoughts will be too!

Therefore, the full extent of a risk has two parts, that can be written simply as:

Risk = probability of collision x consequences of collision

Clearly, the first part is the most important - to have a low probability and <u>avoid</u> a collision. And then the role of the consequences is to influence the <u>safety margin</u> you want on that probability. The higher the consequences the more certain you want to be that the probability is low.

So there is a very practical way in which:

the two elements work together - like a seesaw.

But there is another interplay too, which is less welcome. We have a mental feedback in which <u>fear</u> can reduce control. So bad consequences can <u>increase</u> the probability of something going wrong.

Look at an example. You probably find it easy to walk along a row of kerbstones. The consequences of falling off are low, so you are calm and in good control.

But if instead you were walking along a girder of the same width high on a construction site it would be very different. You would almost certainly fall off - because of the fear of doing so.

Staying in control would take nerves of steel.

In fact, you would perhaps do it better being blindfold and told it was kerbstones!

Therefore, although fear is usually a protective mechanism, it can act in reverse.

On the road too, fear will work against calm control. This is how nervous drivers can get into a spiral if their fears lead to errors, which then confirm their fears.

This makes it even more important to:

**understand risk in a very rational and practical way
that will give you real control.**

2.2.2 Probability of collision

> <u>Key points</u>:   - **Your chance of a collision has three elements: Speed, Surprise and Space.**
>
>   - **You manage risk by keeping these three things well balanced together.**

What a real triumph of technology it would be to have a "probability-of-collision" meter on the dashboard! Like the fuel consumption gauge of a trip computer.

As we learnt how to keep the needle in the green zone, it would teach us safe driving.

It would have to scan the total situation and think ahead, of course:

to catch all the dangers.

And it would need to be accurate, or false alarms would teach us just as effectively to ignore it.

Until that day, though, you must do the job for yourself! And you can - by understanding what is going on in the right way.

Let's look at how crashes happen. At the very basic level, they all need three things:

- something is moving
- something unexpected happens
- someone runs out of room...

Then the impact occurs - it is that simple. Removing any one of these prevents it happening. We can't collide if nothing moves, we don't do it intentionally, and contact is only when a distance comes to zero.

This reveals the fundamental elements in the probability of a collision, which we can call:

Speed, Surprise and Space.

The following table explains each in turn.

Speed seems easy to understand, though is often taken too much in isolation. The key question here is:

"How well can I change speed or direction to avoid danger?"

Braking ability is important, but not just in panic mode - and it is not your only option.

There are also many aspects of speed that are deceptive (as we will see later).

Surprise is less well understood, together with the perils that it brings. The question for you now is:

"How certain am I about everything that will happen next?"

At this stage, we can take surprise to be "anything that makes you do, or consider doing, something before you can calmly check it is safe".

Everything that is not predicted is a potential threat. Having the time to react safely is crucial - not being rushed.

Space is partly understood, though most drivers use it badly. This time the vital point is:

"How much room do I have available to use, and share?"

The concept of "threatened space" is the key, and means recognising what all road users are doing. It is about everyone's need for space.

These three elements form a simple, yet complete "risk model" for the probability of a collision occurring. Increasing Speed will tend to increase risk, and increasing Surprise will too. But increasing Space will decrease risk. So this is easy to remember as:

$$\text{Risk} = \frac{\text{Speed} \times \text{Surprise}}{\text{Space}}$$

This works very intuitively out on the road. If space opens up in front of you, and you are confident about what will happen next, then you are happy to go faster. Or, if you are not sure what to expect, you should drop your speed and/or put more distance between yourself and the uncertainty. And so on.

It works elsewhere too. It is safe to fly in a thin aluminium tube at 600mph, because the planes are kept far apart and the pilots get so few surprises.

But don't try to do mathematics with this model, like double the speed is offset by twice the space, that doesn't work.

It is just:

a logical model of the causes of risk,

and the direction in which they operate.

So, as expert drivers apply their concentration and instincts, these are the essential control levers they use to manage risk - whether consciously or not. And the three elements constantly interact, since changes in any one of them will alter what is needed from the other two.

The model is also a very practical tool. It is easy to remember, and the three elements are things you can think about together, especially with practice. And even more:

it holds true for all situations and all levels of driver skill.

Which makes this a tremendously powerful insight into the dangers you will encounter.

Other people use simple models like this too. All sorts of decision-makers use them to clarify their thinking, and to help them "describe, explain, and predict" the events that they are trying to control. Knowing how things work reduces the chance of wrong decisions being made. And all of this is <u>exactly</u> what we need to do!

It is also clearer now that dangerous situations, or crashes, are not caused by one thing alone, but by the three factors getting out of balance for the circumstances.

So that is the key task - to keep them matched to each other in every situation.

Remember that no single cause of danger can be a viable model for driving.

You are controlling risk when you keep Speed, Surprise and Space in <u>balance</u>.

2.2.3 Consequences of collision

> **Key point:** - **Your margin of safety should be based on how severe the consequences would be if something went wrong.**

Having understood the probability of crashing, we should next think about the safety margin you want on that probability. And this comes from the <u>consequences</u> if a collision were to occur.

Although crashes are often complex, there are typically just two things that are variable at the scene:

- <u>what</u> would be hit

- <u>how hard</u>.

The importance of the "what" is obvious. You want to be even more certain to avoid ploughing into a bus queue of people, for example, than into a wheat field. And if you hit a tree or brick wall, the effect is very different for yourself too. So this is a question about the objects, and how easily they are damaged - or what damage they can inflict on you.

"How hard" the impact would be is about the forces generated, and this comes from the <u>relative</u> speed of the colliding objects. This highlights the difference between hitting something going in the same direction as you, versus something stationary, or even coming towards you. These are crucial distinctions!

This can be remembered as:

Consequences of Collision = objects x impact speed

How much <u>control</u> you could have over an impact once it had become inevitable is difficult to say. Certainly, choosing between alternative things to hit would ask you to think and act very coolly in a split-second crisis.

Any difference you could make, though, might change the outcome dramatically - even affecting your own survival.

And whatever your chances, they will be improved if you:

> think about the severity of potential collisions and let them influence your safety margins.

2.2.4 Summary risk model

There are just three causes of danger that determine the <u>probability</u> of having a collision:

$$\text{Risk} \quad = \quad \frac{\text{Speed} \quad \text{x} \quad \text{Surprise}}{\text{Space}}$$

This is the "basic" risk model that captures the primary aim of safe driving, which is to keep risk low and <u>avoid</u> collisions. Increasing Speed or Surprise will tend to increase danger, but increasing Space will decrease it.

Your start point in controlling risk is to know the three elements: **Speed, Surprise and Space**, and begin to consciously think about them together as you drive. Don't forget, it is meaningless to try to manage risk with just one of them separately - they work together.

> The second stage is then to also think about your safety margins. This will involve the <u>consequences</u> of a collision should it occur. And these, as we just saw, depend on what is hit, and how hard - which we have called the "objects" and "impact speed".
>
> So adding the consequences part gives the "extended" model:

$$\text{Risk} \quad = \quad \frac{\text{Speed} \quad \text{x} \quad \text{Surprise}}{\text{Space}} \quad \text{x} \quad \text{Objects} \quad \text{x} \quad \text{Impact Speed}$$

> Including this second stage, of safety margins, into your thinking is likely to come in its own time, when you are ready for it.

Although this view of danger is quite simple and brief to explain, its implications are profound across your total driving skill. It is central to the whole of your thinking, and each of the five elements needs deliberate attention. You could see them as similar to the basics of the physical side when you first started to drive, which were steering, accelerator, brake, clutch and gears.

So now, in the elements of this model:

> **you have the basis of a very good sense of danger.**

This skill has described <u>what</u> managing risk involves, and the vital importance of balancing together Speed, Surprise and Space.

Taking this further into <u>how</u> to exercise control is explained later in the Risk Assessment and Control skill, which takes each of the elements in turn to examine:

> **how a driver's judgements and decisions about risk can be improved.**

Skill 3: Rules and regulations

> **Key points:** - Any set of rules can only give you a very
> basic ability.
>
> - Ensuring your safety needs many more
> additional skills.

This is the shortest chapter on a skill. Not because it is unimportant, but it is extensively covered elsewhere, with therefore no need to dwell on it here.

You will instantly recognise "rules and regulations" as one of the primary traditional skills - and a very obvious one.

> **Driving clearly needs many rules to organise millions of people into
> sharing the same road network successfully.**

So this skill is concerned with your knowledge of the "rules of the road" - the motoring laws, traffic signs, road markings and instructions for what to do in certain situations.

In Great Britain the material is in the Highway Code and training manuals for the L-test, and there are similar publications in other countries.

> **And this forms a major part of
> initial driver training.**

Brushing up on this knowledge, therefore, is simply a matter of referring back to these sources.

And it is important to do so from time to time, so that your knowledge does not fade or get out of date.

However, then comes a vital point, because no matter how well you know all of these rules:

> they impart to you only a very basic level of ability.

Similarly, when a footballer has mastered all the rules of the game, that only means he is allowed to play. It does not make him a star player. That takes something else. In fact, it takes <u>a lot</u> of something else!

And this shows that there are two parts to your skill here:

- first, the essential <u>knowledge</u> of what the rules are
- and second, understanding their <u>limitations</u> in what they can achieve for you.

If you ask experienced drivers the straight question, "Do the rules and regulations ensure safety?", they will answer a definite "No!". And then probably stop to ponder a little on what that means. Which is, of course, that something else must do it.

> But do not misunderstand. This is certainly not to say <u>break</u> the rules, it is that something in addition is needed. And indeed:
>
> **the Highway Code itself gives us very clear warnings.**

Throughout its rules it says quite frequently:

- "when it is safe to do so...",
- "take extra care...",
- "find a safe gap...", and so on.

> And this, of course, is right at the crucial point of what is going on. Understandably, it is saying:
>
> **"now use your own judgement to make sure you are safe".**

It tells us there is a boundary in what rules can do, and people must think for themselves. No one who writes the rules can be there with you to make sure you are safe. (See also Limitations of Rules in the Surrounding Issues chapter earlier).

There are also more dangerous limitations. For example, we know that speed limits are definitely not safe speeds for all situations. And, more crucially, the rule on safe speed and following distances can lead you directly into catastrophe - if you don't think for yourself (see The Golden Rule, later in the Risk Assessment and Control skill).

> Another vital point is that people often want to feel they will be blameless for what happens as long as they just follow the rules. This can never be true, of course.
>
> **Responsibility for what you do always rests with you.**

Therefore, any set of rules carries two potential pitfalls:

- to imagine that obeying them is <u>enough</u> to guarantee safety
- to expect that they can take <u>responsibility</u> for what happens.

In truth, no matter how elaborate the rules might be, there is not a glimmer of hope that they can cover the infinite variation in real driving situations. That is a false expectation.

And this is why rules alone cannot give you a high level of skill. They are just an elementary start-point, and you should always:

> **use all your other skills to think beyond the rules.**

Skill 4: Learning from experience

Skill 4: Learning from experience

> **Key point:** - Learning is a vital skill in itself - because it builds all your other skills.

Can you really learn how to learn...? This is a good question for any skill. And the answer is that you definitely can - and powerfully so too. This chapter shows how to do it for driving.

Driving experience is usually talked about in years, or in thousands of miles driven. The assumption being that these (almost) automatically increase ability. But this is one of the most obstructive fallacies for gaining skill. In fact:

the years and miles are only <u>opportunities</u> to learn.

And the learning itself may be working well or badly. This helps to explain the wide range of ability among even the "experienced" drivers on the road. Some of them seem locked into repeating the same mistakes year after year, with skills stuck in first gear. Indeed, many older drivers perform worse than younger ones who have better learning.

It is therefore useful to:

recognise the idea of "wasted" experience.

This makes it easier to see that learning from experience is a <u>skill in itself</u> - and can be improved like any other. But with a radically more far-reaching effect!

In a very real sense, and over time, this is your most important skill. Your ability to learn is like:

the "crane that builds cranes",

because all your acquired skill is gained through this one.

Which means it must tower up and span across everything you want to do better.

And no one should duck the opportunity by claiming to be stuck with the learning ability they happen to have. The techniques to improve learning are simple, but very powerful. And progress can be all the more rapid just because people rarely try it.

Fear not, either, if you have a poor memory. This is not about the sort of learning that memorises static facts, to be mechanically recalled later. Both the purpose and the methods are very different. Here we are concerned with understanding how events work dynamically, and relate together.

This is much easier for the brain to do, which is why many of the techniques for memorising <u>facts</u> involve making up <u>stories</u> or mnemonics, for the brain to latch on to.

We can also see that learning from experience is made all the more crucial because the L-test is such a basic standard, and so few drivers take further training. It is a striking omission that drivers are not given more solid guidance on <u>how</u> to learn.

Certainly, the process of:

> **"learning alone" is totally different to learning under instruction.**

But still no one points the way. To say "just keep practising" is to deceive the unsuspecting novice, and does nothing to promote a <u>learning culture</u> that could last a lifetime.

Clearly, skill is not going to come instantly, no matter how powerful the techniques you use. But you can certainly very quickly alter the rate at which you learn.

And that is the aim here - to radically increase your ability to learn.

2.4.1 Seven steps to better learning

<u>Key points</u>: - **Your ability to learn can be readily improved, just like any other.**

- **Learning should focus on what goes right too, not just on your mistakes.**

Here are seven steps to raise your learning ability. And do not be put off by how obvious some of them sound - they still work:

1. **decide to learn**
2. **learn naturally, don't force it**
3. **assess yourself objectively**
4. **find the learning events**
5. **look for why things happen**
6. **use the skills structure**
7. **enjoy what you are doing!**

1. Decide to learn

This may be a bigger hurdle than it sounds, especially for someone trying to bridge from an inactive habit to being fully and actively wanting to learn.

It is a deliberate decision to increase your skill.

The idea is to implant into the way you drive a searching for things to learn. And then to never stop using it. Don't forget that this is what sets apart the way that all experts operate.

This is where you take more active control over your ability.

Recall also from the Driving Process, that "Learning from Experience" is:

the only practical feedback you get to build and reinforce your armoury of skill.

And you should expect that your learning will concentrate in the thinking processes that make your driving decisions.

2. Learn naturally, don't force it

In the quest for high skill:

natural learning is the most effective and enjoyable.

This is the learning capacity we are born with, and the way the brain prefers. It means relaxed and calm, not stressed or forced. And it will find its own pace.

If you approach learning from experience like a classroom cramming exercise, as if for a test, the strain will block the process.

In exactly the same way that "trying to concentrate" creates effort that defeats itself.

Instead, if you just steadily bring your attention to the right things, the learning will happen naturally, by itself.

Don't imagine, either, that you can only learn by pushing hard at the boundaries of your ability. This just creates higher risk. It is like building up normal muscles and physical fitness.

Steady progress is made by avoiding damaging strains.

A brief story will help - about reverse parallel parking. Because this is notoriously very tricky, pupils are taught a thorough procedure of exact start position, and how and when to use each of the controls - handbrake, footbrake, clutch, steering. Careful note is taken of what should be aligned with what at each stage, in a painstaking series of steps. But still many drivers never grasp it well. The actions remain difficult to learn, or to perform accurately.

With our daughter, we tried something different. A zoo close by had a huge overflow car park, totally open except for a few trees at one end. We chose a day when it was totally empty. Starting in the middle, I just asked her to "Drive backwards". Nothing was said about how to control the car - just go backwards. She could already drive well forwards, of course.

At first it was chaos, as expected, and nothing went right. But she persisted in the voyage of discovery. And gradually it began to work. In fact, surprisingly well. Within half an hour she had worked out for herself how to drive backwards - and enjoyed every minute of it. Control and confidence came steadily. We went straight, did turns, figure-of-eights, parked between the trees - anything she fancied. Just driving backwards.

The learning was natural and relaxed, and with fun and pride too as the skill was mastered. It was a powerful and intuitive process, in three stages: trial-and-error, find what works, then practise it over and over. From seeing and feeling what the car did, she was adjusting it to the result that she wanted. It was direct and spontaneous control, by making a deep connection between events and the brain.

We returned over the following weeks for more practice. But when it came to reverse parking, there was no need to think through any steps. The task became to simply: "put the car in the space". Notice that this was then a decision about what to do, not how to do it. This is real driving, not just working the controls.

Two years earlier, with our son, it had been even easier. As an infant he had a pedal-car, and enjoyed riding it around the paths in the garden. Forwards and backwards - wherever he wanted. In the real car I reminded him of those days, and he discovered that he could already drive backwards quite naturally. This included the delicate parking manoeuvre - which had also been part of his games as a child.

Learning that is "result-oriented" is very effective.

But the point here is not that everyone should find a big car park or have a pedal-car as a child. It is that the way we learn is very important to the skills we end up with. Thus learning to drive backwards, rather than just how to park. The intuitive skill becomes much deeper and more flexible than the simply instructed one.

3. Assess yourself objectively

Being able to assess yourself objectively is a theme that runs throughout this book. And it is fundamental to raising any skill.

But excluding bias can be the part that gives trouble. Although, in fact, it is pointless to be anything except objective, especially since:

the assessment is in the privacy of your own head!

People with high skill usually assess themselves quite well. But it can be harder for anyone who is not practised at it.

The trick is for:

> **part of your thinking to remain
> detached and aloof from the task,**

and to calmly monitor what is going on.

This is another defining trait of experts - their detached reflection on their own performance. Not as a destructive criticism, but searching for fine-tuning and ways to do even better.

You should be able to:

> **freely notice mistakes and find the lessons in them.**

And don't think of this as having to "admit" mistakes - instead just <u>notice</u> them. Any focus on "blame" will build a defence against seeing and accepting what can be learned.

In trying to be objective, some people find it helps to adopt a "virtual coach". This is to imagine a friendly trainer is in the car with you. But again, only to help, not to criticise. You may choose it to be someone you know, whose driving you respect.

This will greatly magnify your awareness of what you are doing. (And will only warrant a visit to the psychiatrist if you start talking to them!)

4. Find the learning events

Trying to just "learn all the time" is not very helpful. And it is more useful to identify:

> **specific triggers to clearly signal <u>when</u> to learn.**

There are four main triggers that you can readily use:

- **Errors you make**

  This is the obvious one, and where everyone will tell you to focus. We should hope that big errors will already be grabbing your attention. But you should also pick out increasingly minor ones - the things you may have been telling yourself you can ignore.

  Some people say the best learning experience is when you give yourself a fright. Well, that's quite a scary idea in itself! As we said before, experience is a very poor teacher if we only learn from crashes or near misses. In fact, the best way to avoid big errors is to learn from the small ones. So be prepared to find many "errors" as you begin to seek them out more actively.

  The aim is to virtually tune out errors completely. Indeed, a sign of definite progress is to be working with progressively smaller ones.

  You should quite quickly reach the point where an "error" is:

  > **"anything that allows more than a
  > negligible risk of collision".**

  It might be a decision or action you took - or failed to take. Or it might be failing to observe or anticipate something else that affects you.

- **Surprise!**

  At the higher levels of skill, this is probably the most potent trigger of all, and again shows the power in the concept of "Surprise". It includes here:

  anything that matters that you did not predict,

  and especially any of your own actions that did not turn out as expected.

  Again, expect to find a lot of surprises as you get better at spotting them. You should increasingly get down to including smaller and smaller ones.

  Notice everything that interrupts the calmness of your decisions, and the smoothness of your actions. This is where you will discover <u>what matters</u> in your driving, and the things you are missing that determine safety.

  What makes surprise an especially powerful technique is that it gives "instant feedback", which is the best process for good learning.

- **Errors that others make**

  The popular reaction when someone else makes a mistake is to say, "Well, I hope they learned something from that!". But if it stops there, it is a missed opportunity.

  We can all learn from everyone's mistakes.

  In fact, it is often <u>easier</u> to learn from things other people do wrong, because the learning is not blocked by a sense of guilt or denial.

  Another advantage is that the people around you will (hopefully) be making more errors than you are - which offers more opportunities to learn.

- **Things that go well**

  This is vital. Trying to concentrate hard on only errors is a killer for your motivation to learn. It is wholly negative, and very depressing.

  But if you also focus just as hard on what goes well, you can:

  restore the balance and incentive.

  Any self-sustaining mental process needs a reward - a positive incentive. And this is it for learning.

  Simple examples may happen with your anticipation. On seeing a threat ahead, you hold back. And the situation plays out exactly as you expected... Savour the moment!

  You should especially also note the success of turning habitual mistakes into things that work well instead.

  All of this is your natural motivator to press on, and holds the secret to inspiring a genuine "life-skill".

5. Look for why things happen

The strongest lessons are in <u>why</u> things happen, far more than in just <u>what</u> happens. So, for example, "I took that bend too fast", is worth less than, "I failed to spot the adverse camber".

As we saw before:

finding the <u>cause</u> gives a more useful solution than
seeing only the symptom.

It means that learning to just "not do that again" has less value than changing how you came to decide to do it. There is a more significant and far-reaching effect.

Yet again, this is the way of experts. They do not see just events, but always work back into what makes them happen.

6. Use the skills structure

In Defining the Skills earlier, we built a very meaningful framework for your brain to slot things into (refer back as necessary):

- The "Driving Process" gives a clear shape to the overall task, showing all the parts and how they fit together.

- And "Skills and the Learning Curve" defines the individual skills, and therefore the structured topics for learning.

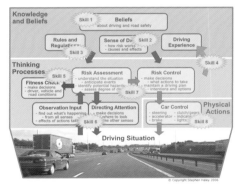

Using the other thinking skills can help you to understand why things happen, and draw the right conclusions. For example:

- **Beliefs** - gives a strong and personal grasp of what is right
- **Sense of Danger** - explains how risk works, and is caused
- **Observation** - helps you to notice more of the things that matter
- **Risk Assessment and Control** - shows the basis of good decisions about what actions to take.

The crucial point is that:

learning is difficult if the mind sees only a random jumble.

It works far better when it can "make sense" of things, seeing patterns and associations in what it is dealing with.

Making sense of the world is a natural and always urgent function in the brain, to which it willingly devotes a lot of its power. And it is no accident that "making sense of things" is exactly what the thinking skills of driving do so well. It gives much more grip to your ability.

7. Enjoy what you are doing !

Last, but by no means least, it is absolutely essential to let yourself enjoy what you are doing.

Recall that this is also in the Beliefs skill.

And the powerful safety reason is that it is impossible to sustain a voluntary interest in anything that your mind is not naturally attracted to.

One of the strong aims of this book, therefore, is to set up a virtuous spiral of:

**enjoy it - do it better
- enjoy it more...**

It is about sparking off a self-feeding motivation that just runs and runs...

This is quite a dense chapter, with a lot to digest and begin to use. And it may help to come back to it a few times.

Don't forget that as with all skills, although someone else may guide your way:

learning is ultimately a very personal endeavour.

And the aim is to create a process of learning at the very heart of your everyday driving.

With this achieved, every journey becomes a totally natural training exercise for all of your future driving.

Learning is the engine of skill. As we said at the top, it works as the "crane that builds cranes".

**This is the skill that will give the strongest
acceleration in your ability.**

Skill 5: Fitness check

> **Key points**: - Before you drive, double check whether you should.
>
> - And also as you continue to drive too.

This is about <u>whether</u> you should drive, rather than <u>how</u> you drive. It sounds like a very simple decision, and it should be.

But a lot of drivers get it wrong.

And by no means just those who do so <u>deliberately</u>.

Every day millions of people take to the roads with very little thought. And the aim is to not be one of them. (How to cope with the drivers who are the thoughtless ones is in the rest of this book!)

It is true that poor judgement here can be easy to mask if it is not too blatant. And of course, something else may then be quickly blamed for any mishap. But that doesn't really help.

Most of this chapter should be well known to most drivers, and the question is likely to be how far they still ignore it.

So this is the second of the three chapters that are already a major part of current driver training and education. (The other two are Rules and Regulations, and Car Control).

The main value here is in:

- bringing a number of things together in the same decision
- raising your thinking to a more conscious level
- highlighting that, as with other decisions, good Observation and Risk Assessment are needed here too.

As we saw in the Driving Process, there are three elements to be assessed:

1. are <u>you</u> fit to drive?
2. is the <u>vehicle</u> fit to drive?
3. are the <u>roads</u> fit to be driven on?

The criteria are covered in the Highway Code and motoring regulations, and supported in various ways by publicity campaigns and law enforcement.

However, although it may be tempting to do so:

> **your decisions should not be based solely on**
> **what is "legal" or could be "proved".**

The risks run far beyond that, and any misjudgement just loads your task with a self-inflicted handicap.

Also important is that your decisions are not made only as you start off, but throughout the journey too. And that you are able to respond to any changes, such as becoming tired, suspecting a mechanical fault, or a severe change in the weather.

2.5.1 Driver fitness

> **Key point**: - **Most errors in the decision to drive involve how drivers assess themselves.**

The question here is simple:

> are you always genuinely fit to drive when you get behind the wheel?

There is mounting evidence that failures here are claiming far more lives than previously thought. The main issues are in eyesight, drink and drugs, fatigue and anger management.

Let's stress again that "legal" or "provable" are inadequate criteria, and you should always think for yourself beyond that level.

2.5.1.1 Eyesight

It is a scary prospect, but:

> millions of drivers do not meet even the legal standard

of being able to read a number plate at 20.5 metres (67 feet). Most estimates are around 5-10% of drivers, though some are higher. These people bring danger wherever they go. And while eyesight usually gets worse with age, many young people are affected too.

However, the test for driving eyesight was devised a lifetime ago, back in 1935, and in modern traffic is woefully inadequate. Out on the road, this standard is now far too poor for seeing the detail that allows you to pick out the emerging threats - especially in complex situations or at higher speeds.

No one should assume that eyesight is blameless in a crash simply because it is legal.

A much better standard for safe vision is 2-3 times the legal distance, and that means:

> **reading a number plate at 40-60 metres, or more.**

If you have good vision, try an easy experiment.

> Pace out 20.5 metres from a car in good light, and screw up your eyes so you could just about tell a police officer the right characters on the number plate.

> Now notice how little detail you can see, especially into the distance beyond the car, and imagine someone driving like that along a busy motorway or city street.

Not only is this legal, but millions of drivers are doing exactly that, plus thousands more who are <u>even worse</u>. The test also misses other problems, such as tunnel vision that makes any moving around a bit tricky.

This should raise your level of concern about eyesight. Driving with defective vision is blatantly reckless, possibly worse than being drunk. The point is blindingly simple:

> **without good eyesight, you can't be safe!**

And no one should hesitate to see an optician. Most defects are easily rectified, and it might save a life you care about!

2.5.1.2 Alcohol and drugs

This is about:

> **chemicals in the blood that distort decisions in the brain.**

For many people, alcohol is the best known issue in this chapter. Amounts in the breath and blood are easily measured, which has helped it into high profile.

> The legal limits are vigorously enforced, with high penalties available to the courts. Some statistics are:
> - nearly one in seven deaths on the road involves a driver who is over the legal limit
> - drink-drive crashes kill or injure 20,000 people a year
> - at twice the legal limit you are at least 50 times more likely to crash.

The problem is worst on Friday, Saturday and Sunday nights, and mainly with younger people, though still significant up into middle age. Judgement is altered:

> **mainly by creating overconfidence and slowing reactions.**

Drugs have been more difficult to detect than alcohol, though that is changing. And don't be misled by the political moves to decriminalise some recreational drugs. This has nothing to do with approving them for driving. The effects on judgement remain the same.

But illegal drugs are not the only problem. It is also true that:

> **many legal medicines affect the ability to drive too,**

and it is important that drivers read the labels on medication, and consult a doctor or pharmacist if in doubt.

Driving under the influence of any drug that impairs your ability is <u>predictably</u> dangerous. Like alcohol, the effects are often to slow down reactions and/or to raise confidence.

2.5.1.3 Fatigue

Drowsiness at the wheel is now thought to cause about 10% of all road casualties, and 20% of serious crashes on motorways and monotonous roads. However, estimates vary widely because momentary sleep is hard to prove. But precision is not needed to see this as a big problem.

> Too many drivers are nodding off at the wheel, and some do it repeatedly.

And in the crashes, the absence of pre-impact braking creates severe injuries - with a high percentage of fatalities too.

> A dramatic case occurred in February 2001 in the Selby Rail Crash, that killed 10 people and injured 70 more. The verdict was that a driver had fallen asleep in the early morning, and plunged off the M62 on to a rail track in front of two trains.

> Perversely, there was an outpouring of public sympathy for the driver. An alarming number of drivers admitted that they too had fallen asleep at the wheel, and claimed it was a genuine "accident" because it could happen to anyone.

> This was denial of responsibility on a huge scale! But the driver's sentence showed no such sympathy.

Everyone should be totally clear:

> falling asleep at the wheel **is** under a driver's control.

It does not happen without ample warning and a prolonged period of fighting off the drowsiness (except in very rare cases). So the decision to continue driving is a deliberate one. Even the 1% of drivers who suffer from the "obstructive sleep apnoea" disorder do know that they are fighting sleep

To some degree, we can all choose when to sleep, but eventually it is not a matter of choice. The strongest willpower to stay awake will be overcome, and often at that point, quite suddenly. Tired drivers will often "micro-nap" without being aware of it. You may be able to spot their unusual road positions and jerky steering action.

> But it is also very wrong to believe that falling asleep is the only problem.

> You don't have to fall asleep
> for fatigue to impair your driving.

High risk factors include:

- type of driver:
    - young male, aged under 30 years (more overconfident)
    - truck drivers, company car drivers and shift workers
    - those deprived of sleep, or awake for more than 20 hours
    - anyone with a diagnosed sleep disorder
    - anyone on medication that induces drowsiness

- time of day:
    - when the body and mind normally expects to be sleeping
    - after a heavy meal
    - in the troughs of the body's natural biological clock:
        - early morning, 2-6:00am, has a very high risk
        - mid-afternoon, 3-4:00pm, has a slightly raised risk

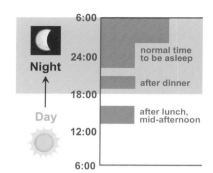

- type of journey
    - long and without breaks
- type of roads
    - motorways and trunk roads, where boredom comes from low visual stimulation, the steady drone of the engine, and a lack of driver activity
- other risks of drowsiness come from: ill health, alcohol and drugs.

Notice that, in addition to biological tiredness, drowsiness can also occur from boredom and low stimulation.

In combating fatigue:

most of the common tactics are ineffective.

They include opening a window, taking a short walk, turning up the radio, talking to a passenger, etc. It may be effective for up to 2 hours to drink 150mg of caffeine (about two cups of coffee) combined with a 15 minute nap. But even this is much more risky than taking proper sleep. The research shows clearly that:

fatigue <u>avoidance</u> is much more effective.

Widespread recommendations now include:
- plan the journey to avoid times when you would normally be asleep
- rest well before long journeys, and take a short break every 2 hours
- set the ventilation to give cool fresh air at face level
- be aware of the high risk factors above.

But still most important, is to <u>know</u> your own condition, and to act on it.

Driving while too tired is something we can definitely put on a par with drink-driving for being wilfully reckless. It cannot be passed off as being beyond a driver's control.

All drivers should "wake up to drowsiness"!

2.5.1.4 Anger management

This is usually a danger that occurs more during a journey than at the outset. And:

if anger flares up, it can quickly render you unfit to drive.

You will radiate high risk by being aggressive and unpredictable.

We touched on emotion and aggression in the chapter on Beliefs, and there is a strong link with "Surprise" too. You may be angered by behaviour on the road that you see as a territorial challenge, but if someone surprises you it can have the same effect. This is because surprises tend to feel threatening, so you might find yourself wanting to object.

But whatever the cause, if you give vent to your anger you start on a spiral towards a full blown road rage contest, with a wide spectrum of threats.

Deliberate attacks might develop, or even a murderous intent.

Certainly, anger is a natural reaction to threats that you feel unable to control. But it is also true that:

it can be triggered by something quite trivial.

And how important can anything be with someone you just pass in the traffic, and will never know? Most definitely, if you want to teach them something, the strongest lesson of all is in self-restraint.

Having said that, controlling anger can depend on your disposition, and some people find it more difficult than others. Though we all must do it somehow. And you can make it much easier by deciding beforehand that you will:

- share road space, not claim it as territory
- use good anticipation to accept calmly what others do - even their mistakes
- apologise if you make a mistake
- not take things personally, and therefore not "seek revenge"
- never assume the other person will back down - that in itself is an escalation
- always hold control over the situation, and not see that as submitting.

In most human confrontations, sufficient signals are given between the parties to avoid coming to blows. But if this fails, the threats can escalate into an explosive attack.

Once the adrenalin starts pumping, it takes over judgement and actions.

Here are some tips to put you in control of conflict:

- limit movement to appear non-threatening. Being over-animated signals aggression
- offer a calming gesture of conciliation and closure - an upheld hand, with relaxed palm outward
- a slight smile will confirm the lack of harmful intent - though laughter may seem to be mocking
- look away, perhaps with head slightly lowered. This is the opposite posture to an attack
- avoid hard eye contact. A direct stare is aggressive, and will enflame most situations
- put space between you and the other person. This is one of the most basic and successful ways of coping with danger
- remain calm, look where you are going and drive normally.

The key is to:

recognise <u>now</u> that you will someday
meet events that make you angry,

and decide in advance how you will deal with it. Then, as it happens, remember that holding control of the situation, and preventing an escalation is the only real success.

Use brain not brawn to cope with anger.

2.5.1.5 In summary

There will probably always be some struggle in admitting to being unfit to drive when you want to. And two points are vital as you decide. You must be able to:

- see yourself <u>objectively</u>. It may help to imagine you are making the decision for someone else - a driver you might meet on the road
- consciously <u>reject</u> any pressures to press on regardless that swell up from the ego, or other people, or just a tight time schedule.

2.5.2 Vehicle fitness

> **<u>Key point</u>:** **- Every time you drive a car, your safety depends on it being roadworthy.**

This is about the safety of the machine you drive - including any load. In law, ensuring that the vehicle is roadworthy is the driver's responsibility. And it cannot be passed off to anyone else, such as the owner or a garage that does the servicing.

It sounds simple enough, yet not everyone takes it seriously.

In a random survey in 2001, 12.4% of vehicles failed the legal standard, and 7.4% were stopped from driving on.

If the police are called to the scene of a crash, the vehicles are always examined for any signs of contributory defects. Especially if casualties are involved.

The responsibilities are well known, and listed in places like the Highway Code and vehicle handbooks. They include tyres, brakes, steering, lights, windows, etc, etc.

Within this, there are things that a garage should do, and others that drivers are expected to do themselves. But it especially falls to the driver to:

pick up faults that develop while driving.

Also at this point comes adjusting the car to the driver. This includes seatbelts, seat, headrest, steering wheel, mirrors, etc. They affect comfort, alertness, vision and your feel for the motion of the car.

A common mistake in seat position, especially with nervous drivers, is to set it too close to the wheel. This restricts arm movements, and also risks being hit hard by a deploying airbag.

Mirrors are often badly adjusted too (see Blind Spots, in the Observation chapter). The adjustability of mirrors is both their best and worst feature. They should be set for you.

2.5.3 Road conditions

Key point: - **Although the weather can be unpredictable, to come under an extreme threat from it will usually be caused by a bad decision to drive.**

This decision is about the effect that the weather has on road conditions. And it has three parts: grip, visibility and high wind.

Again, the dangers are very well known, and the decision should be an obvious one. But it is easy to see how:

people get caught out when they push the limit.

For grip, the road surface is affected by:

- rain (especially after a dry spell)
- ice
- snow
- flood

And for visibility, the problems are:

- fog
- torrential rain
- thick falling snow

High wind has dangers in:

- blowing vehicles across the road
- trees and other objects falling into the road.

Coping with extreme weather includes:

- getting the forecast whenever it could be a threat
- being prepared to interrupt a journey if necessary
- taking any equipment you may need, such as shovels, towrope, mobile phone, etc.

And remember that poor weather can quickly affect your ability to see into the distance, and therefore to assess risks and respond to them early. Which brings us very neatly to the Observation skill, next.

Skill 6: Observation

> <u>Key points</u>:　- **Observation is a critical skill - but it is about <u>understanding situations</u>, not just seeing objects.**
>
> - **It means noticing what is relevant, and actively directing attention.**
>
> - **Poor observation is shown by surprise.**
>
> - **Better observation stimulates higher attention.**

In the Driving Process, we called poor observation the "secret error". Because it is not a physical action, it is often less obvious than other mistakes.

But it plays a major part in nearly all crashes - even when they are blamed on something else.

Indeed, the drivers themselves will often not be aware of what they failed to notice that could have prevented their crash.

So by exploring how observation really works, this chapter explains how this can happen. And, more usefully, shows also how you can prevent it happening to you.

It starts right at the beginning with what observation means and how we perceive things at all. A new definition is given for what we mean by a "hazard", followed by a number of specific techniques for improving observation.

Earlier, we identified that:

Observation is one of the two most vital skills,

(the other one is Risk Assessment and Control).

Let's begin by being very clear about exactly what observation is - no matter how obvious it might seem to be already. We will also discover how to measure how good it is too.

2.6.1 Notice more

Recall the Observation cycle from the Driving Process.

You gather input from the driving situation, and use a risk assessment to direct your attention.

This is the fastest spinning loop in the driving task.

Recall too, that it does not include deciding <u>what to do</u> about what you observe. That comes later.

2.6.1.1 Definition

So now, what do you think "good observation" means? Is it really as simple as just "looking where you are going"? Whatever it is, out on the road it becomes clear that most drivers have powers of observation that are not particularly good. Interestingly, at the scene of a crash:

it is very common to find that someone
"looked but didn't see".

Everyone agrees that observation is critical, but "looking" gets confused with "seeing", and then also with "understanding". Neither looking nor seeing are enough, without understanding the significance of what is there.

In terms of human evolution, of course, modern traffic is a very new kind of phenomenon. Never before has there been a need to keep track of so many moving things so intently, and over such distances and for such long times. Even our primeval hunting skills are working very hard as we do this.

Nonetheless, we all know people who float through life missing much of what goes on around them. Even things they see mean little to them, and it limits their sense of experience. On the road, though, the consequences are serious.

The purpose of observation, as we saw before, is to:

collect the information needed to make the
right decisions about what to do.

And this must include all of the senses, not just vision. Hearing and the sense of motion are also necessary inputs.

The word <u>notice</u> is vital in observation - especially in the detail. And then, what is noticed must be relevant too, which requires you to interpret what it means.

Compare two observations of a bus:

- "the bus in front is red and new, with an interesting poster for skiing holidays on the back"
- "the bus in front is going quickly, but some passengers are starting to rise from their seats".

Or a school girl:

- "the school girl on the path has a smart grey uniform, and reminds me of my own daughter at that age"
- "the school girl on the path is excited at having just spotted her friends in the playground across the road".

These may all be accurate observations, but the contrast shows vividly the meaning of relevance. The first views have taken our attention, but give nothing back for our driving. The second cases have found useful points for risk assessment. The bus is likely to stop sharply, and the girl may run into the road.

Now we can add that good observation includes:

> **noticing what is relevant to your safety,**
> **as early as possible.**

Remember that observation is the <u>only</u> way to sense what is happening. Without being clairvoyant, there is no substitute!

But clearly, no one can pay attention to everything all of the time. The brain soon hits a limit on what it can handle. Even more, though, people often let their attention wander quite aimlessly, without being conscious of where it is.

And this means that:

> **the decisions on where to put your attention**
> **must be quite deliberate.**

Over time, doing this more consciously will build a stronger intuitive sense of where to focus.

You should expect too that these decisions will always be balancing the search for new risks against tracking the ones already found. This is why they are guided by risk assessment.

The most common faults in directing attention are:

- "attention drift" and allowing distractions
- "looking too short" - typically less than 30 metres
- "fixating" - usually on the vehicle in front.

2.6.1.2 Measurement

Could it be possible for drivers to "measure" how good their own observation is...?

A practical measure offers itself in the form of one of the three causes of danger - Surprise. It is not precise, but can be very useful.

The basis is that a failure in observation is signalled by:

> anything important that you did not predict would happen.

This will certainly highlight when you miss events that could lead to danger.

You can also fail to see static things like road signs, of course. But if your observation spots everything that avoids surprise, you are likely to be seeing these too.

Recall that surprise is also one of the strong triggers in Learning from Experience. And again this shows the skills working well together.

So nearly every surprise starts as a failure in observation. For example, having to brake sharply may result from not spotting 5-10 seconds ago the slowing traffic in the distance. Or if you miss a cyclist's glance over the shoulder, their move across the road will look very sudden.

> Something unexpected happens <u>because</u> we failed to pick up the early signs of it.

Learning from a surprise, no matter how small, starts by asking, "What <u>could</u> I have noticed, to have let me expect that...?". Whatever happens, there is nearly always a warning indication somewhere. More on this in the Surprise topic later.

As observation improves, your surprises will very quickly get less severe and less in number. But do not be tempted to claim success by just ignoring them. Or by just blaming someone else for acting suddenly. That would simply resign you to poor observation.

2.6.1.3 Reward cycle

Another important benefit of good observation is its "reward cycle".

Once a driver's attention emerges out of its vagueness:

the habit of noticing more will spark a renewed interest in the task.

This in turn will attract a higher natural concentration - and a virtuous cycle continues.

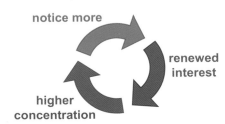

2.6.2 Perception and deception

> <u>Key points</u>:
> - **The brain constantly makes observation errors by taking shortcuts.**
> - **The biggest driving problem is when it "stops looking" for danger.**
> - **And this is only overcome by being consciously alert.**

Usually, we have to assume that we see the world correctly, and act on it. Otherwise we would do nothing. But in truth, all of your observation is only a bunch of "perceptions" in your head. And:

> they don't always match what is really out there.

The old adage "perception is reality" shows the problem precisely.

Imagine you pay a shopkeeper with a £20 note, and receive change from £10 as a genuine error. You are in for a heated dispute if the £20 note is not still separate to be inspected.

In a single "actual reality" there are different perceptions - and actions.

The same happens when arguing blame at the scene of a road crash. Even allowing for the biased motives, there can be:

> sincere but conflicting beliefs about what truly happened.

And this probably also caused the crash in the first place. In the classic rear-shunt at a roundabout, for example, the second driver is totally convinced that the first one moved off. But they didn't!

Alongside this, the human mind it supremely keen to make sense of things, and this is one of its most intense and automatic functions. This is why most of us want to feel a sense of order before being ready to move on to something else. Conversely, the eccentricity of artists and innovators is often rooted in an unusually high tolerance for chaos and meaninglessness.

But in trying to make its best guesses from the jumble of input it receives:

> the brain can be easily deceived.

"Magic" shows and "illusionists" play artfully in this area. And although optical illusions are amusing, they do have a serious side. Even your desires can fool your perception too!

Here are some common deceptions. They are mostly subconscious, and the effect on activities like driving is profound:

- **Selectivity**

  The sheer volume of sensory input to the brain means that most of it gets ignored, by constantly deciding what to "tune out". As you read this page you are not aware of feeling your foot in its shoe, the taste in your mouth, or what is in the corner of your vision. (But now you are!)

  Perception is <u>very</u> selective - according to
  where your attention is.

  This protects the mind from colossal overload, and derives deeper meaning from what is selected. Subconsciously, the mind is simply drawn to what it finds most interesting. But the attention can also be directed very consciously.

- **Familiarity**

  Very high selectivity occurs when the mind tunes out things that are constant, well known, repetitious or predictable. Such as normal noises around the house.

  But it also happens with habits, such as tailgating, where:

  drivers can become unwittingly adapted, and
  lose sight of familiar dangers.

  It stops when risks are assessed more consciously.

- **Constancy**

  Even more, the mind <u>prefers</u> to create constant and simplified perceptions - as a defence against a world that is complex and stressful. And this has pros and cons.

  It certainly helps events to seem reassuringly stable and orderly, and stops us having to examine every object and situation as if for the first time. But conversely, reacting to the unexpected then takes longer.

  If a pedestrian steps straight out in front of you:

  part of your reaction time is the vital instant in which
  it is "unbelievable".

  And the same happens when any road user makes a really blatant error - unless you have consciously accepted the possibility beforehand.

- **Monotony**

  In addition, losing alertness is a natural response to monotony. Without the stimulation of change, our senses actually shut down. And drowsiness is induced without being tired. Steady speed in a cosy car are ideal conditions for this to occur.

  Similarly:

  taking little interest in any task also leads to
  a state of mind-numbing boredom.

  Which is why we see so many drivers with a slumped posture and vacant expression. Giving the mind something to work on keeps it active.

- **Expectation**

What you "expect" can be one of the strongest deceptions, as the anticipation in the brain overrides the input from the senses. In looking for the easiest path:

the mind tries to fit events into its expectations.

Have you ever recognised someone you had arranged to meet, only to call out to a stranger? Or have you failed to spot a change in a road you know well until the very last second? The mind is always tempted to make lazy perceptions.

- **Optimism Bias**

There is also an involuntary bias towards seeing what we <u>want</u> to see. And we prefer to believe that all is well, even if it means seeking comfort in denial when it is not - especially if the problem is our own fault!

Many risks on the road are taken by simply assuming that all is well.

- **Herd Instinct**

Perceptions are also very "infectious". There is a compelling pressure to discard our own perception if other people seem not to share it. In many ways, this conforming influence helps us live in civilised harmony, but it also spreads bad practices too. And thus:

you may find yourself driving as if in a herd.

Too fast in fog, or too close at speed - just because everyone else is. Driving is an intensely group behaviour, and the transmission of perceptions is very strong.

The key point here is not to learn these deceptions. But simply to recognise the flaws, and to know how vital it is to be acutely alert.

The spiral into monotony, for example, is quickly reversed by taking more interest.

Just thinking more about your driving will naturally stimulate your observation and return you to vigilance. In fact, it can even become a little addictive.

Apathy, of course, runs the cycle the other way.

To stay alert, the mind needs to have enough to think about!

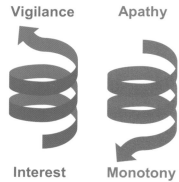

Vigilance   Apathy

Interest   Monotony

2.6.3 Defining hazards

> **Key points**:   - You are part of every hazard you meet.
>
>   - And this is what gives you control !

"What is a hazard?" is a vital question. Focusing properly on danger includes being able to separate the real threats from the unreal ones. And this starts with what you regard a "hazard" to be.

We saw before how crucial the activity of Directing Attention is to good observation. No one can give their full attention to everything all of the time, so selecting what is important is the key. Without this, you will spot the genuine dangers much later, when they have become very obvious and harder to handle.

Traditionally, a hazard is defined as:

> *"Any situation which could involve adjusting speed or changing course."*

And there are variations on the same theme. But seeing a hazard like this has two drawbacks:

- it is too general to help you identify which risks need your attention
- it portrays the problem as something that is "out there", that you "react to".

Certainly, after basic training, a driver should not have to regard every need to change speed or direction as a hazard. Most evidently, keeping pace with a flow of traffic and following ordinary bends in the road should be performed as a safe routine. The term "hazard" should be reserved to pick out actual dangers.

In re-thinking this, the first thing to recognise is that, for all the dangers you face:

part of the hazard is **YOU !!**

This is not an accusation, but the simple fact that a collision is a meeting of two objects. And remember also that you can only prevail over danger by thinking beyond who is to blame for it.

So, your hazards only exist because you are there too, and in that sense it is helpful to shoulder some responsibility for letting them happen. This might seem a bit hard on you, but in practice you will meet very few situations where it is not valid to some degree.

But this should not be depressing at all. It is actually very good news, because:

this is what gives you control !

The fact that you <u>are</u> involved allows you to change the outcome. This is a cornerstone of "defensive" driving, though for most drivers it is a radical shift in thinking about their hazards.

It also highlights that you don't have to wait for threats to become significant. There is far more skill in preventing danger, rather than simply responding when it has become urgent. And predicting where danger will arise is done with your powers of Observation and Risk Assessment.

Returning to "What is a hazard?", a good definition will point you to what needs your attention, and will also show that you are <u>actively</u> involved and exercising <u>control</u>. Thus, a sharper focus comes from seeing a hazard as:

> **"Any threat to you, that is**
> **not already allowed for in your thinking and actions".**

This promotes a more useful grasp of what is happening, and leads you to:

- assess the magnitude of risks, so the real threats stand out
- consider whether you have done enough about them
- look specifically for things you are <u>not yet prepared for</u>.

This is not to totally ignore what you <u>are</u> prepared for, of course, but to accept that it needs less of your attention. By being prepared for how a threat could develop, you reduce the risk it carries. For example, by giving an erratic driver a bit more space, your attention can then include searching for other dangers too.

Often simply being alert to a danger can reduce it. For instance, knowing how to spot when someone will change lane suddenly in front of you.

It is also clear from this, that hazards are not the same for all drivers, and:

> **a bad driver will be part of worse hazards than a**
> **good one in the same situation.**

Lastly, remember too that hazards do not line up neatly and separately, to come one at a time. They often overlap in a chaotic jumble, with more than one needing to be tracked at once. This is why placing your attention is such a vital and continuous decision.

2.6.4 What to look for

> <u>Key points</u>:   - **Your own thinking should decide what needs your attention, not a list of things someone told you to watch out for.**
>
>   - **Anything you may need to react to is important, especially if it reduces your control over what will happen to you.**
>
>   - **Treat the surprises you get as observation failures.**

It is impossible to list what you should look for in every situation you will meet. And you will already have been told the obvious things anyway.

Instead, this section is about how to discover for yourself what really needs your attention as you drive.

Later, when we look at the biology of seeing, we will also discover a certain basic skill in simply not stressing the ability of your visual equipment.

But as the brain wrestles to interpret its vast inputs, there is an even bigger problem in the sheer quantity of information it can realistically take in.

So there is a very practical need to:

decide where to
direct your attention.

This is definitely a major skill that you can build up to make a huge difference.

Clearly, as danger constantly comes and goes, observation is dramatically improved by knowing how to pick out what is important. Drivers who can do this will understand far more about what is really happening.

And even more, there is something crucial in any threat about:

how much <u>control you have</u> over

the way that events unfold.

2.6.4.1 Types of threat

Let's take some types of threat as examples, and see how they affect your control over what happens to you. Starting with the worst one:

- **Definite threats**

  These are probably much more common than you would wish. They exist where:

  > you have very limited control over
  > whether a collision will occur.

  The control may be with someone else, or surrendered to luck. These are situations that could force you into sudden strong action.

  > The car in front is a definite threat whenever emergency action would be needed if it braked sharply.

  > A driver behaving erratically close to you is probably a definite threat too.

  > The question is:

  > > "how much control are you happy
  > > to let others have?".

  Strictly, we should also count the vehicles coming towards you on the other side of the road - until you are satisfied that they are being driven under control.

  Definite threats can also be things that could make your own normal actions dangerous, such as a car riding tight up behind, or someone who has not seen you.

  And even more vitally, if your control is reduced because of your own actions, you may want to reconsider what you are doing!

  > All definite threats must be tracked intently
  > until they are resolved.

- **Potential threats**

  These are threats that hold early signs of reducing your control. They will usually:

  > need you to take some action, but not suddenly.

  You still have calm control, but a definite threat is likely to emerge if you fail to use it. For example, a car overtaking towards you in the distance may need you to slow slightly to give a little more space. Or you may position to go a bit wider past a wobbling pedestrian late at night.

  And even stationary objects can be potential threats if you pass so close as to need extra care.

- **Indirect threats**

  These are certain to be happening all the time, and occur when:

  > a danger to someone else could make them
  > react and become a threat to you.

  You are unlikely to hit the original danger, but it could make you hit something else.

For example, if a child might step out in front of a vehicle coming towards you, then that is an indirect threat - because the vehicle could swerve into a head-on crash.

Or, imagine you are the blue car in this motorway scene:

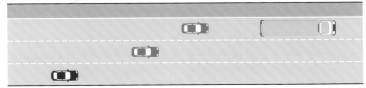

There is indirect danger from the red car in the inside lane. If it suddenly pulls out to pass the lorry - or even just indicates - the green one might swerve into your lane just as you are about to pass. Having seen the risk you can think about how to diffuse it - perhaps by just holding back until the green car has safely passed the danger. Note how quickly the danger can transfer across the lanes.

And so indirect threats require you to:

notice when people around you are in danger,

and consider how they might react. It is one step beyond the obvious threats, but is a very powerful part of your observation. It will spot risks early, and where they start, which puts you in maximum control. But it does involve casting your attention beyond the closest objects.

- **Stationary threats**

 How dangerous can a stationary object be? Well, if it stays still it should be okay - assuming you don't misjudge everything and drive into it anyway!

 However, because the strongest function of vision is to <u>detect movement</u>, stationary objects can easily fade into the background. So we should give particular attention to things that <u>could move</u>, as well as the ones that are already moving. The car standing at a junction, the child waiting to cross the road, the parked car with people inside - threats like these can be "invisible" in busy traffic.

 Also, moving objects are usually easier to anticipate. Their observable speed and direction give good clues about what comes next. But:

 when something is just starting to move
 it can be harder to predict.

 Which has the greater potential for danger, cars passing you normally on the other side of the road, or the ones parked along your side that may have people inside? The parked cars have a "hidden" danger of pulling out or opening a door without warning. Notice that parked cars with their front wheels turned out are the ones that can move off easily.

 However, there are ways in which even stationary or slow moving road users can betray their intentions. When every moment of warning counts you should:

 - **look at vehicle wheels** - the slightest rotation is very obvious, even the first few inches. It shows exact speed, and even the rate of acceleration. If you can see the front wheels, they will show the intended direction of travel too.

Be aware, also, that if an oncoming car is waiting to turn across your path, it is a greater threat if the wheels are turned than if they are still straight with the road.

- **look at pedestrians' legs** - people usually shift their weight or raise a leg slightly in preparation for stepping forward. You should not need to wait until you see the whole body moving.

- **notice where people are looking** - for all road users this is often the direction in which they will move. It may also show you whether they are distracted. If necessary, do not be shy about sounding your horn to alert them to your presence.

- **notice people's intentions** - by knowing what people want to do, you can also see whether it would create a hazard if they started to do it.

2.6.4.2 Every surprise

We said that good observation is about "noticing what is relevant to your safety". Even further now, it is:

> noticing anything that might create
> a need for you to react.

When assessing how good your observation is, we know from before that "surprise" is a good indicator of failure at some level. It shows exactly when something important was missed, and probably what it was too. In fact, this is another view of reduced control, because it highlights things you were not prepared for.

How to control and avoid Surprise is covered in its own major section later, and it is also a key trigger for Learning from Experience. But the important point here is to:

> ensure that your observation does not overlook
> when a surprise has occurred.

Two things should help:

1. **Notice your surprises objectively**

   Being objective about your driving is stressed a number of times throughout this book, and it does get easier with practice. The trick in your observation is to actively look for anything that you didn't predict would happen.

   If a cyclist in front, for example, swerves and makes you react, then they have surprised you. Especially to begin with, you may well find a lot of surprises going on. And their potential consequence will show how serious they are.

   Also, if your decisions or actions feel even slightly rushed, it is another sign that you are reacting to something unexpected. Clearly, all surprises are not equally important. But:

   > a surprise is only "minor" if you can
   > cope with it calmly and smoothly,

   and with only a slight change to what you had previously intended to do.

2. Identify the causes

This will make a very big difference. It is finding whatever you could have noticed to avoid being surprised.

If the swerving cyclist above did so to avoid a puddle, then you would have expected it if you had noticed the puddle!

This is, after all, one of the things that cyclists do.

Nearly every surprise has a detectable warning somewhere. And even the slightest clue can be vital. If you can find it, and lodge it firmly in your mind.

Doing this consciously will build your observation skill very quickly.

In addition, the real power of identifying causes is in showing:

how to recognise where surprises <u>might</u> come from.

Suddenly your observation is transformed from a "reactive" sense, looking at what has already happened, into a "proactive" one that stimulates thinking about what <u>could</u> happen next. So potential dangers will be far less unexpected, and if they happen you will be prepared - or might even have already taken the action required.

But still, don't expect to eradicate every surprise completely. The objective is to reduce them to only the ones that pose no threat.

Depending on where you are starting from, your powers of observation might improve quite dramatically. And as they do:

be prepared for your driving style to change too.

Expert drivers, for example, need far less unplanned braking than others. And the braking they do is earlier and lighter too. This flows naturally from their observation that helps them anticipate and plan ahead very effectively.

Even so, expect it to take some time to firmly lodge any new habit into your driving - there is no instant magic switch. But:

**when sharp observation becomes second nature
the payback is huge.**

2.6.5 Limitations of vision

> **Key points:** - **Many crashes include someone who "looked but did not see" some vital part of what was happening.**
>
> - **Vision is a massively complex sense, and should only be trusted with care.**

This section covers the vital, but rarely considered, strengths and weaknesses of your vision itself:

- the biological realities
- facts about dim light and glare
- how we see motion and distance.

No one needs to be reminded that vision is the most important sense for driving. Yet we rarely spare a thought for what a stunning feat it is.

Tiny shafts of light enter the eyes, and magically become the most vivid awareness imaginable. We see a vast array of objects, surfaces, edges, patterns and brilliant colours. Plus, a spellbinding sense of movement and space. Truly amazing - inconceivable if we didn't see it with our own eyes!

But:

even good eyesight falls far short of the
perfect sense we expect it to be.

Just as we saw with perception, there are vital limitations that we ignore at our peril.

Discovering what they are begins with a basic understanding of the equipment - the visual system itself. And the first jolt is that, although we think of "seeing" with our eyes, that is not what really happens.

At best it is a half-truth, and scientifically it is very wrong. The meaningful sense of vision is built in the <u>brain,</u> not in the eyes. And the role of the brain is at the heart of our grasp of how vision works.

Of passing interest are the attempts to give a full vision sense to machines. The optics and control mechanisms of the "eyes" are the easy part. The much tougher challenge is in how far the electronics can produce the "visual brain" functions.

Let's look at both parts: the eyes, and then the brain.

2.6.5.1 Eyes - the optical instrument

For our purpose, the eye is just an optical instrument. Light shines in the front, and is focused on to light-sensitive cells at the back. Human eyes are typical among animals. They are quite simple, and basically unchanged from our tiny mammal ancestors of 50 million years ago. Many insects, for example, have much more complex arrangements.

Of the various parts of the eye, we are interested in just three - that may be recalled from happy school days!

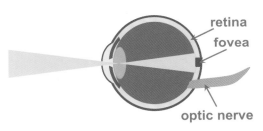

- **Retina**: the layer of millions of light-sensitive cells, creating signals for the brain.

- **Fovea**: the central and most sensitive area of the retina, the size of a pinhead.

  This is the only point where vision is sharp and colourful.

  It sees a circle about one centimetre in diameter on the page you are reading, which equates to the front of a car at 70 metres.

  We use this area to examine things closely. Away from this small point the detail and colour degrades quickly into our peripheral vision.

- **Optic nerve**: runs out of the back of the retina, carrying signals to the brain. But it leaves a small place on the retina that has no light-sensitive cells at all. And this creates a blind spot on the retina and in the visual field of each eye - that we have learned to ignore (see Blind Spots later).

In addition, the retina is made up of two types of cell - **rods and cones**, that work very differently:

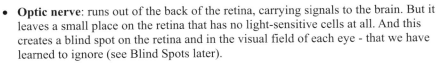

Rods	Cones
• see only <u>shades of grey</u>, and <u>vague detail</u>. Very <u>sensitive to movement</u>, but <u>slow to respond</u>.	• see <u>clear colour</u> and <u>sharp detail</u>. Respond <u>quickly to movement</u>.
• work well in <u>dim light</u>, but are <u>overwhelmed by bright light</u>.	• work well in <u>good light</u>, but become <u>blind in dim light</u>.
• are located across the whole retina surface except in the fovea.	• the fovea is totally cones, but they thin out quickly into peripheral vision.
• these are the original sensors, dating back to primitive nocturnal creatures. Bats and owls still have only rods.	• these cells evolved later, and give our rich sense of vision.

This helps to explain how the eyes perform in the four different light levels that cover most driving conditions:

Bright Light - comfortable daylight:
- ideal conditions
- our best vision (given by the cones)
- crisp detail, and bright colours
- good sensitivity to rapid movement.

Half-light - early evening:
- vision is harder to trust
- many "tricks of the light"
- rods and cones are working uneasily together
- identified by when car colours are turning to grey.

Dim Light - moonlight or darker:
- shapes and detail are vague, and in shades of grey (only the rods are working)
- sensitivity to movement is still good, but slow
- loss of detail gives poor judgement of movement and distance (try playing catch with a ball by moonlight!)
- the central spot of vision sees nothing, except for any points of brightness
- more than 90% of visual input can be lost compared to good light.

Dim with Headlight Glare
- spots of glare affect large areas of vision
- sudden brightness causes a stabbing pain
- temporary blindness as the eyes need a few seconds to adapt between each moment of glare. This adapting takes longer with age
- eyes tire more quickly from constantly adjusting between extremes of light
- the main technique is to avoid looking directly into the oncoming headlights
- blinding sun in daylight can have similar effects.

A crucial point is that, although the eyes can handle a very wide range of brightness or darkness:

the adapting process <u>takes a long time</u>.

And also, they cannot handle extremes of bright and dark together in the same scene.

This means that, in anything other than good light, there is an unavoidable struggle for your vision and observation. And following it right the way through, the effect is:

a driver with delayed reactions and poorer anticipation.

Notice especially that the way the eyes perform is completely a biological fact. And no amount of bravado or pretending can make them into better instruments.

Our skill here therefore is in:

using our eyes safely as they are, by adjusting to their limitations.

2.6.5.2 The brain - imagining vision

Although the eyes are simple, our brain is the most elaborate on the planet. And in vision, which is the most spectacular of our senses, a huge amount of processing power is applied to the raw signals from the eyes. More of the brain is involved in vision than for any other function - about half of the highly developed part that looks after conscious experience (the cerebral cortex).

Such power is needed for two reasons. Firstly, the vast stream of data from millions of cells in the eyes must all be processed in "real time". In fact, the job is broken down into unbelievably small pieces for massive parallel processing. It is the most amazing dissection and reconstruction of a problem you could ever imagine.

Secondly, even this amount of data is not enough to construct the full sense that we have. And it transpires that:

our memory supplies <u>more</u> information than comes in from the eyes!

This gives faster processing and enriches the sense by taking shortcuts and filling in any gaps.

How we see cartoons shows this capability very well. From just a few sketchy lines we can instantly see objects, and even recognise faces.

Babies cannot do this, because they lack the memories.

Even more, the secret of most optical illusions lies in tricking the brain - not the eyes.

Usually, this complex process in the brain does a fairly good job - which is how we come to trust it. But we can now appreciate that:

the trusted experience of vision is far less direct than people think.

However, among all this relentless turmoil, there is another cautionary tale that is even more bizarre - and telling. The parts of the brain that process the elements of <u>vision</u> are essentially the same parts as are active for <u>remembering</u>, <u>imagining</u> or <u>dreaming</u> the same things. So the brain actually has quite a fine line between its real and imaginary worlds.

The possibility that someone could genuinely "imagine they saw" something is now easier to understand. And this also graphically underlines that:

**the brain is very able to "cover up" for any
holes left in our casual observations.**

(You will see this happening later in a little exercise in the Blind Spots section.)

So, as we jump into our cars and venture out to dodge around each other in thick traffic at high speed, we should know that the brain will create for itself much of the detail that we fail to notice ourselves. This helps to explain why it is so common to "look but not see".

How far your vision sees the real world depends on
your conscious efforts to provide the input.

2.6.5.3 Seeing movement

Having explored the role the brain plays in how vision works, we can now look at what it achieves - starting with how we see movement, and then distance and space.

Our eyes are <u>very</u> sensitive to movement. Motion is a defining part of life, and the more something moves, the more "alive" it seems to be. Even average eyesight can spot ants on a wall at 10 metres - if they move.

The eyes are also <u>attracted</u> to motion, with an automatic reflex to turn and look - to check whether we have to react. In the survival contest of evolution, this works very well. But now in driving, this reflex is hugely overloaded, and is numbed in the process.

Even so, it is still true that:

seeing movement is the visual system's
most critical function.

However, the brain receives <u>four</u> conflicting components of visual movement, which it must juggle and resolve into a single interpretation:

- images sweep across the retina as the objects move
- the eyes move in the head, also moving the images
- the head moves on our shoulders
- the whole body can be moved through space.

How can it possibly work out what is going on? This is another hugely complex problem that we ask the brain to solve very quickly.

Clearly, for example, when your eyes flit from one thing to another, and your head turns to track an object, while you are also driving along through the traffic... you must still know what is actually moving, and what is not.

To adjust for your own physical motion, the brain also takes input from the balance organs in the inner ear, and the sensations in your limbs. This is how you can run without losing stable vision. But the motion of driving has very little physical sensation, so the brain has to rely even more on the eyes.

Naturally:

all of this does not happen perfectly all of the time!

You get dizzy if you spin round then stop - because what the eyes see conflicts with the liquid in the ears that is still moving. Fairground rides and flight simulators also confuse the senses quite easily about what is moving and stationary. And have you ever been in a traffic queue, and felt for a moment that you were rolling back when the car in front edged forward?

Now let's look at the two basic types of motion that we observe, and how we assess them. Unfortunately:

**the motion that is more threatening is also
the one that is harder to detect.**

* **Side-to-side motion**

    This is very easy to notice, because there is a lot of change in what we see, even on small movements. So if a car 50 metres away moves 1 metre to the side, the motion is obvious. Assessing any movement <u>across</u> our field of view is very good.

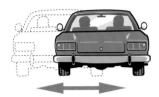

* **Away-towards motion**

    This is harder to detect, because there are only slight changes in the image - just slightly bigger or smaller. If a car 50 metres away moves even 5 metres closer or further away, it is barely noticeable.

    Unfortunately, of course, the biggest threats come from objects travelling straight towards us (or us towards them). So it is important that when the car in front shows its brake lights, it takes quite a time to assess how hard the braking is.

    For the task of driving, therefore:

    our detection of away-towards motion is <u>not</u> very good.

All of this means that misjudging movement can happen quite easily - especially if your attention is weak. And this severely affects the next essential job, which is your <u>anticipation</u>, where the brain must constantly cast the motion forward to predict "what happens next"!

2.6.5.4 Seeing distance and space

To move around successfully, requires not only good judgement of motion, but also of distances and spaces too. After all:

the spaces are what the motion must fit into!

And in this endeavour too, the invention of the motorcar places higher demands on our ability than nature had in mind.

This time, the challenge for the brain is to get a three-dimensional meaning from images in the eye that are essentially flat. Having two eyes helps a lot, but much more than that is needed. And:

we instinctively look for as many clues as we can find.

A lot of distance indicators are used:

* **Stereoscopic vision**

    Because they are a few inches apart, our eyes see slightly different pictures, and the brain interprets this into distances. The effect is very strong for near objects, but is ineffective at more than 100 metres away.

- **Motion parallax**

  Even slight head movement makes objects at different distances appear to move across each other. Distant hills on the horizon appear to move behind things that are closer to us. This is a very strong clue about how far away things are. And because it involves us moving, it should be extremely useful in driving.

  However, there are also two weaknesses:
    - there is no effect for things that we travel directly towards
    - it is easily confused if the object is moving too.

- **Relative position**

  Objects that can be seen to be in front of others must be closer (obviously!)

- **Vertical position**

  When looking at a landscape that is fairly flat, objects further away touch the ground higher up in the picture. This is another strong indicator.

- **Size constancy**

  We already know the normal size of many things, such as cars, so the size of the image we see shows how close they are. But this only works for standard objects.

- **Perspective**

  Parallel lines look closer together into the distance - such as the edges of a road, etc. Evenly spaced lane markings or cat's-eyes also seem to get closer with distance.

- **Sharpness**

  Because the air is not perfectly clear, objects get less distinct into the distance.

  Edges blur, details merge and colours fade into pale tones. But this is only useful into the far distance.

  Artists use this to create a feeling of great depth on a flat canvas.

- **Scene knowledge**

  In familiar places we use known objects as reference points. Being in a familiar place when a major feature, such as a building or tree, has been removed is confusing until the memory is changed.

Again, seeing distance and space uses a lot of brain-power. And there will often be conflicts among the various indicators. Indeed, there are very striking optical illusions that show just how easily the brain can get confused by input that appears to be inconsistent.

So inevitably:

> **tricks can be played on your sense of distance and space, especially if attention is low.**

2.6.6 How to look

Key points: - **Looking effectively at a driving scene is less obvious than you might think.**

- **But some simple techniques can make a big difference.**

"How to look" sounds like a crazy title. After all, you have been looking at things all your life, and must surely know how to do it by now!

But this is exactly the problem. Looking at a driving scene is very different to most things you look at, and most drivers treat it too casually.

For driving, your looking must be the start of a chain of full observation, which is "looking-seeing-understanding". And this, in turn, begins to prepare you for making those life-or-death decisions about the actions you will take.

It needs a different way of looking - more focused, and extracting more information. Even more focused than being glued to a football game or window shopping around town!

So the problem is that:

> drivers are sure they know how to look, but then do it badly.

Older readers may recall the pedestrian kerb drill before the current Green Cross Code. "Look right, look left, and look right again", was drummed into school children as a memorable chant. However, they then executed it as a chant too, with a rhythmic head turning motion before lunging into the road no matter what. It was replaced because the children were pointing their head, without actually <u>looking</u>!

For adults, the danger is very similar - that information is not even being received. So don't be tricked into thinking this does not matter. Nothing else in observation, or beyond, can work if you do not begin by looking effectively.

2.6.6.1 The commanding view

The first essential is a good view forward. That is where most of your dangers will be. We could say:

> you need a "commanding view" over the situation
> you are driving into.

This means having a view that gives you clear sight of all the hazards, so that you can plan well ahead.

Achieving this requires active adjustment to your road position. And this is a major part of how you use the road space available to you - although most drivers fail to do it. Getting the right lines of sight is crucial, and helping you to "see and be seen" is a key Purpose of Position (see later in the Space section).

Drivers most commonly sacrifice their commanding view by:

- being so close behind a vehicle that it blocks their view - especially when behind large trucks, vans and MPVs
- driving exactly in line with the vehicles in front, with no view past them
- in multi-lane traffic, allowing other vehicles to block the view of junctions.

In thick traffic, slight bends are excellent for giving a longer view of what lies ahead. Straight roads might seem safer, with no steering to do, but the obstructed view is a deceptive danger that causes multi-vehicle pile-ups.

Clearly, though, a commanding view is not always possible. And you must also, therefore, be sure that you:

recognise very positively when you do not have one!

2.6.6.2 All-round awareness

The next priority, after your view forward, is good awareness all round.

Many threats will come at you from behind or from the sides. From behind, you have tailgaters, and people wanting to pass - including cyclists in slow traffic. And on the sides there are junctions and the traffic alongside you.

The need for all round awareness may be most obvious when you are slowing or moving across other traffic to execute a manoeuvre, but threats can occur at any time.

Any gap in your awareness is a risk.

So knowing what is happening all around you should be a constant aim - even if it is sometimes hard to achieve.

There was an extreme example of blinkered awareness in a television documentary in the mid-1990's. It showed an elderly driver on a motorway who deliberately never looked behind.

Stubbornly, he explained, "I should be looking forward. People behind should be looking out for themselves".

And to support this he cited that if someone hit him from behind, then legally it was their fault, not his.

To make matters much worse, he also refused to drive faster than 50mph, so always had a heavy flow of traffic coming past. High risk on a number of counts!

But what do you think of faster traffic behind you? Have you ever not seen it coming, and been startled? It does you no good to berate the driver under your breath for pushing a bow-wave of surprise in front of him. The only control you have is to be more vigilant.

Mirrors should be used all the time, not just when manoeuvring.

Now let's consider what you <u>can't</u> see. This is often more critical than what you can see, because the risks are harder to assess - and often get ignored. Recognising where you cannot see is vital to total awareness.

One of the most overlooked parts of observation is:

to know which parts of your situation you know too little about.

You should try to "feel" the blindness created by things like:

- a blocked line of sight, whether due to other traffic, such as a passing lorry, or part of the landscape, such as a bend, brow of a hill, building, etc
- poor visibility from fading light, or bad weather, etc
- places where you could see, but have not looked for a while. Typically, it might be when you have been tracking a specific threat. But as you do that, the pressure should be mounting to check again all round.

This then prompts a decision to switch your attention, or adjust position to open a new line of sight. Even while giving serious threats extra attention, you must still beware of ignoring other parts of the scene for too long. There is no point in avoiding one hazard, only to create another.

Your physical <u>blind spots</u> are also crucial, of course, and are covered later in this chapter. There are two types - the ones around your vehicle, and the ones in your eyes.

2.6.6.3 Peripheral vision and awareness

This is even more strongly about <u>how</u> to look.

The reason we look <u>directly</u> at something is to see it accurately. But your peripheral vision gives you an awareness that is wider than that. This is invaluable when we move around, and the question in driving is:

how much use do you make of it?

For most people, peripheral vision extends to a little over 180 degrees. Right round to slightly behind you. It increasingly lacks colour and detail as you go wider, but is very sensitive to movement right out to the edge.

But wide <u>awareness</u> does not come automatically from having wide vision.

Just as some people have a medical disorder of tunnel vision, it is easy to get an attention disorder of "tunnel awareness". This means that your attention is focused narrowly, and to the exclusion of the wider picture.

tunnel awareness

peripheral awareness

cyclists
pedestrians

Peripheral awareness means:

genuinely <u>noticing</u> a wider field.

Widening your awareness is not difficult, and you do not even need to be driving. In fact, it may help to start with if you are not.

Try an exercise while watching television. Without looking away from the screen, notice what else is in the room. Start close to the set and work outwards. Everything is just waiting for your attention to find it. See how much you can notice while still following the programme. When someone in the room moves, can you tell what they are doing? Confirm for yourself how well you can detect movement.

You can also practise in safe moving situations, such as walking around shops or down the street.

Take in more of what lies to the sides, without having to look directly at it all.

Move confidently between people, knowing where they are and judging their movement without

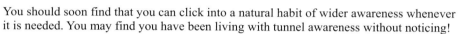

looking straight at them all. Extend awareness on both sides at the same time.

You should soon find that you can click into a natural habit of wider awareness whenever it is needed. You may find you have been living with tunnel awareness without noticing!

But you don't have to try to capture the full 180 degree angle suddenly in one step. Even half way out will be a huge benefit. Remember, though, that the aim is to <u>increase</u> your field of awareness, not to use the periphery as a distraction. You must still:

> maintain awareness of the main thing you are looking at directly.

And just as importantly, neither is peripheral awareness an excuse to drive with a fixed stare - see Scanning below.

2.6.6.4 Scanning

If you look at the drivers around you, you will see how many of them seem to be locked into a mesmerised stare - probably glued to the vehicle in front.

This is:

> the disastrous habit of "fixating".

Even the fixated object is not seen well, because the brain is shutting down out of sheer boredom. In this state, anything at all that happens takes longer to register.

So good observation relies on scanning, which means:

> actively searching for sources of danger.

Your eyes should be moving nearly all the time, checking different parts of the scene.

But this does not mean randomly gazing around, nor moving the eyes in a wild mechanical pattern! Scanning should be an intelligent searching, that is guided by:

- the dangers you are already tracking
- experience of where other dangers might be
- completing coverage of the whole scene.

It is part of:

directing your attention to ensure nothing is missed.

Again, let's stress that scanning and peripheral awareness are not alternatives. They complement each other, and should be used together. Think of peripheral awareness as searching with a wide beam torch instead of a narrow one. And then by scanning, you will still move the torch around, but see more wherever it goes.

Scanning is also about looking into the distance, not just from side to side across the foreground. Some trainers call this:

"raising your vision" - looking up and into the distance.

It is good practice to scan into the distance before looking away from forwards, such as into the mirrors or at the speedometer. This checks that it is safe to spend time looking elsewhere.

Scanning promotes alertness too, by stimulating the brain's thirst for input. In contrast, fixating is a form of sensory deprivation, that leads to boredom and a mental shutdown.

2.6.6.5 Gazing and glancing

How long does it take you to look into a mirror, or to check your speed? For how long are you not looking where you are going?

On average, drivers take about 1 or 2 seconds, perhaps longer. At best this is a significant loss of time, or at worst it might be longer than their following distance to the car in front.

Critical events happen in much less time, and the level of risk can rocket while you are looking away.

The problem is that:

we tend to "gaze" until the image has registered its meaning.

But this is rarely necessary.

1 sec

2 secs

Most times the purpose is to just check whether something is close behind, or confirm our approximate speed. For this, there is no need for a detailed study:

a quick "glance" can tell you what you need
in a much shorter time.

Try it with your watch to see what is possible. Cover it with a hand, then reveal it and cover it again quickly. Your brain will capture the image in very short exposures, and still make sense of it. You can probably do about 1/10th of a second if your hand is that quick, and still know what you saw.

There is no need to try for anything near 1/10th of a second glances while driving, of course. But you can dramatically shorten the normal "looking away" times. Moving your head slightly as well as your eyes might also help.

The single needle of a speedometer is an even easier picture than looking in a mirror. Especially since you know roughly where it is anyway. You may want to take a bit longer in a speed camera zone, but the point is still valid.

In 1998, a television campaign called "Julie" was launched, aimed at getting rear passengers to wear seatbelts. It showed a mother driving her children to school.

A van behind caught her eye, and she looked in the mirror for quite a while, only to look back just as she ploughed full tilt into another car. Her son in the back, without a seatbelt, was thrown forward and killed her.

The punch line was about the son not wearing the belt. Unfortunately, the <u>cause</u> of the crash was not mentioned, which was that she had looked behind for far too long.

The main value of rapid glancing is:

> **when the situation is tight ahead, but you**
> **still feel a need to check elsewhere.**

Ideally, you would not be this short of time, but modern traffic often denies us that luxury. And even without a specific pressure in front, there is still no reason to have your eyes off the road for longer than is necessary. If the quick glance shows that a longer look is needed, then you can prepare for it and choose your moment.

With practice, using short glances when appropriate will capture enough information. And this is a good way to maintain all-round awareness with little sacrifice of the front view.

There is no need to change suddenly, though. You can try it occasionally, and:

> **gradually take less time looking away.**

2.6.6.6 At night and in poor visibility

One of the main points earlier in Limitations of Vision was that the biological working of the eyes is a given fact. Beyond wearing glasses to correct medical defects, we cannot change the basic way that the eyes work.

Therefore there is a skill in:

> **how we cope with situations**
> **that the eyes find difficult.**

So night driving, for example, is more than just flicking on the lights and driving as we do in daylight.

The eyes see much less detail in darkness - <u>and</u> more slowly too.

And the problems are not confined to failing light. They include any low-light situation, such as unlit tunnels or a dark avenue of trees, and also glare from headlights or badly aimed security lights, etc.

To this we can also add poor visibility from the weather. Rain, snow and fog all make it more difficult to see. In combination, such as driving in the rain at night:

> you may commonly lose over 95% of the useful vision you have in clear daylight.

It may be tempting to ignore just how much our driving needs to change in these circumstances, but your powers of observation are reduced in specific ways:

- **Failure to see** - this is the most obvious effect! The harder it is to see, the more likely you are to miss something important.

  People often think of "looked but didn't see" as happening in good daylight, but the danger is, unsurprisingly, higher when seeing is difficult in the first place.

- **Poor judgement of speed and distance** - a lot of the detail that is lost is exactly what we use to accurately judge motion and position. Our decisions, therefore, are working with a much weaker sense of speed and distance.

  And this includes a vaguer sense of your own speed and precise position too.

- **Poor anticipation** - when so much input is lost from the lack of visual detail, it is inevitable that your anticipation will suffer badly.

  Good anticipation relies totally on picking up the small signs and early warnings that are no longer available.

- **Temporary blindness** - glare can create a severe loss of vision for a while. And it may not always be practical to avoid looking into bright lights.

  Some people find it helps to close one eye when dazzled, so that it recovers more quickly. But be aware that your judgement of distance and speed is likely to be very poor indeed during that moment.

- **Eye strain and fatigue** - any form of struggling to see, or looking towards intermittent headlights, will cause particular stress on the eyes.

  In addition, it also accelerates fatigue, which will threaten your attention level too. This is especially likely if you are driving at a time of day when your body is expecting to be asleep anyway.

These are all very real problems in observation that you must deal with, and one of the essentials as you do this is to:

> stay focused, and allow yourself <u>more time</u> to look and see.

2.6.7 Blind spots

> **Key points**: - **Never forget your blind spots.**
> - **The hiding places are always there.**

No one needs to have the importance of blind spots explained to them. The dangers of not seeing something are self-evident. But a chapter on observation would not be complete without a quick run through the problem.

Again, this is:

> **a vital part of being acutely aware of what you <u>cannot</u> see.**

There are two types of blind spot:

- around your car   - an obvious risk
- in your eyes   - a less well-known effect

2.6.7.1 Around your car

As you sit in the driving seat, you have a number of blind spots. These are the places you cannot see by looking forward, moving your head easily, or using the mirrors.

They will be approximately as shown below, though will vary for each car-driver combination - and will, of course, be reversed for left-hand drive cars.

Let's look at each of them, going clockwise from the front:

- **Driver windscreen pillar**

  This is the most lethal blind spot, being so close to the direction of travel. And:

  it can be quite wide.

  Behind this pillar is exactly where traffic comes towards you on the approach to roundabouts and junctions.

  It also hides oncoming vehicles on fast right-hand bends.

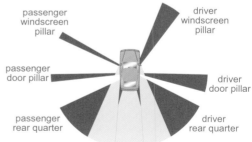

The pillar varies enormously between car designs. Sometimes it intrudes quite noticeably into the field of vision, and its width also has a very strong effect.

Because human eyes are about 7cm apart, we can "see around" obstacles that are up to this wide, and close to us. But the hidden area grows quickly above 7cm. For example, a 9cm wide pillar creates twice the blind spot of an 8cm one. Unfortunately:

> *even some modern cars have very wide pillars.*

When the windscreen is sloped back, either for aerodynamics or styling, this pillar must be even stronger. And it is not uncommon to find them up to 12cm wide. This can hide a pedestrian just 6 metres away, or a whole car head-on at 20 metres!

Sacrificing vision for style seems a peculiar trade, and perhaps something to notice when buying a car.

Especially, be aware that this blind spot creates severe crashes with motorcycles as cars emerge from junctions. The bikes have a thin profile, but travel at normal traffic speeds. A good technique for drivers is to simply look twice. For their own safety:

> some bikers call this the "killer pillar".

- **Driver door pillar and rear quarter**

  This is probably the next worst problem. It is critical in common situations, such as overtaking, changing lane or turning right. Even the "life-saver" glance over the shoulder, can leave a large area unseen.

  > A poorly adjusted door mirror will
  > dramatically increase this blind spot,

  perhaps by something as simple as leaving it where another driver has it set.

- **Passenger rear quarter**

  In theory you could see this area by swivelling right round to look out of the rear side window. But this is so far round from the forward view that:

  > turning to look is risky at speed or in thick traffic.

  This blind spot can be a problem when turning left or changing lane. Again, the unseen area is increased by having the passenger door mirror badly set.

- **Passenger windscreen and door pillars**

  These are narrower blind spots, and far round from the line of travel. But they can still block the view of traffic as you emerge from some junctions.

But with all of these blind spots, there are several ways you can overcome the dangers:
- maintain good all round awareness, and:

  > notice when something <u>moves into</u> one of your blind spots
- be prepared to:

  > move your head or look twice when necessary,

  especially to see round the driver windscreen pillar.
- be aware that the best thing about mirrors is also the worst thing about them too - they are adjustable.

  > Set mirrors to maximise the useful vision.

  Failing to do this is a common error. The internal rear mirror should need only a slight turn of the head to give a clear backward view.

  And door mirrors should not show you a lot of the side of your car - you already know where that is. They are more valuable aimed wider into the rear quarters.
- fit extra "blind spot" mirrors to the door mirrors to widen the angle of view.
- keep windows clean and sticker-free to avoid creating even more of a problem.

Also remember that blind spots may change - with time of day or the weather. At night it is harder to know precisely what you can see in any of the mirrors. And:

rain will create blind spots too,

by obscuring parts of the windscreen, other windows and the door mirrors. Even a passenger's head will create a blind spot at some junctions.

And finally, having understood your own blind spots, you can also be more acutely aware of where other drivers cannot see - especially if it is where you are! Being unseen always puts you in danger. The counter is to <u>know</u> when you are in someone's blind spot, and try not to stay there. And sound your horn if necessary.

Also be aware that big lorries have a habit of side-swiping cars that sit next to the cab on their passenger side. And watch out for left-hand drive lorries where the blind spots are reversed, since you will pass through this position as you overtake them.

2.6.7.2 Blind spots in your eyes

Many people do not know that they have blind spots in their eyes. They are less visually obvious than the ones around your car.

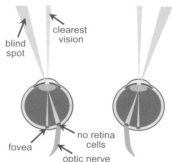

LEFT EYE   RIGHT EYE

As we know, the spot where the optic nerve exits the back of the eye has no light-sensitive cells.

This gives a blind spot, that is about 20 degrees to the outside of the centre of vision, as shown.

But in size, they are:

larger than you probably imagine,

being 1/15th of the viewing distance in diameter.

That means a circle 2-3cm across on a page held at normal reading distance, or the front view of a car (about 2 metres across) at 30 metres.

But these blind spots go unnoticed for three reasons:

- they are in the peripheral vision, not the centre of focus
- the spot of one eye is visible in the peripheral vision of the other one
- the brain itself will fill in the missing piece of the image.

That last point may seem a bit scary, and you will see it happen in a simple exercise below.

In the visual field, these blind spots are about where the blobs are in this scene.

And the biggest problem is that:

you are not aware of them.

They can become a significant threat if:

- your gaze is fixed, and the same part of the scene stays in the blind spot
- the peripheral vision of the other eye is blocked, for example by the driver windscreen pillar. This effectively makes the pillar blind spot wider.

But in case some readers are still sceptical, let's have a demonstration with the picture below. Try these steps:

- in good light, look directly at the picture at a distance of about 30cm
- close your left eye and look at the centre of the blue square with your right eye
- move slowly towards the page until the red circle disappears from your peripheral vision. If you move even closer, it will come back again

- notice how completely it disappears
- and what did you see instead? Not a "hole", but an unbroken yellow background.

The brain is seeing what it thinks it should.

Then do the same but with the truck and the family. Notice that if you look even slightly away from the truck in any direction, the family reappears.

After a while, you should be able to flick your right eye between the blue square and the truck and make the family and the circle alternately appear and disappear!

By the way:

at 30mph you would reach this family in about 2 seconds.

There are many versions of this demonstration, and some wonderfully entertaining tricks you can find on the internet.

You can also try it with your car outside. Stand facing it head on, about 50 metres away. Close your left eye, and this time look straight at the car with your right eye. Now look slowly to the left, until at about 20 degrees movement, the car disappears. Move closer, and try it again. See how close you need to be before you do not lose it completely. It will probably be about 30 metres.

But it is easy to neutralise the effects of these blind spots. You simply need to:

keep your eyes moving and scanning the scene,
and don't let your gaze fixate on anything for a long time.

2.6.8 Seeing round corners

> **Key point**: - A driving scene can tell you a lot more than you immediately see.

Your physics teacher told you that light travels in dead straight lines, not in curves, otherwise it would get jumbled up. However, in practice there are many ways to stretch your observation past the obvious view that presents itself.

In part, this is:

<u>a frame of mind</u> that searches beyond what you can easily see.

Here are some examples, and you will find more for yourself:

- **What others do**

    People transmit a lot of clues about what <u>they</u> can see. If the car in front brakes or moves to the crown of the road as it goes over a blind brow or round a bend - it tells you something.

    If the traffic coming round a bend is unusually slow or tightly packed - that tells you something too.

    These are:

    warnings of a probable danger that you can't see.

    Picking up these signals from the road users around you can extend your "vision" to include some of what they know too.

- **Look through**

    In tight traffic, look <u>through</u> the vehicle in front, not just at it, because:

    you need to know what they are driving into.

    Imagine the driver has only average skills, and may react late to any hazards.

    If you cannot see through, then compensate for the risk by changing position to see past, or backing off further.

    Also, look through hedgerows around bends, especially in winter when they are bare of leaves. And of course, if a bend is open, look across it, and not just at the piece of tarmac you can see.

- **Look under vehicles**

    Large vehicles can often:

    hide smaller ones, such as cars or cyclists.

    But many lorries are high enough to see under.

    Another favourite is children who get off a bus and walk out in front of it before it moves off. Look for the telltale feet under the front corner of the bus.

- **Shadows**

  On a sunny day in tight traffic, if you can't see past the vehicle in front, the shadows:

  may show you if other traffic is there.

- **Headlight beams**

  This is probably the only advantage you get at night. Noticing headlight beams around bends or shining out of driveways:

  can give earlier warning than you would see in daylight.

- **Reflections**

  A view around obstacles is sometimes shown by reflections in shop windows, or even in other vehicles' paintwork. This may be useful in slow-moving traffic in busy streets.

- **Vanishing point**

  The vanishing point of a bend is the farthest point you can see up the road, where it disappears round the curve.

  When this point moves quickly away from you, the curve is beginning to straighten out. Conversely, you know that:

  if you are getting closer to it, the tightest part of the bend is yet to come.

  After a while, how this point moves will become part of the instinctive "look" of a bend, that you respond to naturally.

- **Listen**

  Some vehicles can be heard before they are seen - especially lorries and motorbikes. This may be useful along winding country roads, or in heavy traffic when bikers come through quickly from behind.

  Sound does travel round corners.

  At blind junctions or in thick fog consider opening a window to hear any traffic.

- **Understand the meaning**

  What does fresh mud or dung on a country road mean? Perhaps the tractors or animals are still close. Dustbins lining the roadside might tell you that refuse vehicles are out nearby. A long queue at a bus-stop indicates a bus is due.

  A dense pattern of skids on the road shows a popular spot for heavy braking. And anywhere that has a lot of road markings or barriers signifies a danger that someone has seen fit to spend money on.

  Looking for what things mean:

  reveals another dimension to observation.

With all this added information, though, be sure to use it only for extra warnings, and:

> **not to raise your confidence about things**
> **you should still treat as unknown.**

Don't throw your safety into someone else's hands by assuming they are telling you that something you cannot see is safe.

2.6.9 Other senses

<u>Key points</u>: - **Feeling your movement and hearing what is around you are important parts of observation.**

- **Sensing the motion and stresses of the car is essential to being in full physical control.**

Even though driving would be impossible without vision, there are essential parts of observation that come from your other senses.

Streams of information are available in what you feel, what you hear, and sometimes even in what you smell too. And they will often:

> **give earlier warnings than vision.**

2.6.9.1 Feeling the movement

Whenever you move, you <u>feel</u> the motion in your limbs. And this is what lets you control the movement. In strenuous sports it is intense, but it works the same way for more normal activities too.

Imagine, for example, trying to walk or run while feeling no sensation in your legs or feet.

Similarly, in driving:

> **it is essential to feel the motion of the car.**

Although your limbs are not providing the power to transport you, this is still your direct sense of the control you have over the vehicle.

In fact, you probably underestimate how much notice you take of it already. Without this feedback, driving would feel strangely detached - like floating in a computer game.

So your sense of motion:

> **connects you directly with the car's behaviour.**

It tells you what the car is doing, and lets you know confidently how it will respond to the demands you make on it.

Every point of contact is a source of input - the seat, steering wheel, and even the pedals. Together they let you feel the motion, the stresses on the car, the grip on the road, and sometimes the onset of mechanical faults.

A lot of your <u>speed</u> sensation also comes from what you feel through the car. And it is important to know the situations when this is reduced. Cruising at steady speed, for example, in a modern car on a smooth and straight road, gives a low "feeling" of the speed.

When this part of your observation is firmly in place:

> **the car can become a natural, instinctive and
> <u>predictable</u> extension of the body.**

And that is the only way to achieve full physical control.

2.6.9.2 Hearing danger

There are some things that only sound can tell you.

And they can be crucial, such as:

* vehicles close by, in your blind spots or round corners
* warnings from a horn or emergency vehicle siren
* speed sensation from the general noise level
* a door or tailgate that is not fully latched
* the noise of a flat tyre, or something in the tread
* engine tone indicating stress or faults
* noisy exhaust warns of holes starting
* etc, etc.

You will think of more examples, and what is certain is that:

> **the sounds around you provide a crucial part of total observation.**

2.6.9.3 Smelling danger

More rarely useful, but to complete the picture, smell can help you to detect things such as:

* being close to farm animals or vehicles on a country road
* exhaust fumes escaping into the passenger compartment
* overheating engine
* electrical faults
* slipping clutch
* dragging brakes
* fire under the bonnet
* etc, etc.

Again, you may think of more.

2.6.9.4 Vehicle empathy

How well do you know your car? It may sound like a strange question, but this is also an important part of observation.

Vehicle empathy is about taking sensitive notice of the machine, and:

> **avoiding high mechanical stresses and wear**
> **due to rough or clumsy use.**

In safety terms, the purpose is to avoid straying beyond the car's capability or breaking a vital component at a dangerous moment. You might also like the fact that it will probably save you money too.

This does not mean inflicting a slow or boring style on yourself. Indeed, racing drivers especially know that:

> **driving smoothly reduces risk.**

There is a total difference between working your car as it is intended, and abusing it by being inept and ignoring its distress.

Examples of rough treatment include:

- slipping or jerking the clutch
- forcing or crashing gear changes
- engine revs that are too low or too high
- habitually fierce acceleration, braking or cornering
- hitting bumps or potholes at speed
- kerbing the wheels when parking.

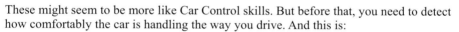

These might seem to be more like Car Control skills. But before that, you need to detect how comfortably the car is handling the way you drive. And this is:

> **an observation skill of feeling, hearing and sensing the machine.**

Certainly, expert drivers intuitively know the level of exertion they are placing on their loyal servant - and exactly what it can be safely asked to do. They <u>feel</u> the engine giving power, the brakes taking it back again, the gentle matching of a gear change, and the tyres gripping to hold a bend - everything it is having to do.

Another benefit is that you are more likely to:

> **detect early signs of mechanical problems.**

Potentially lethal faults in brakes, tyres, steering, suspension, etc, are often preceded by a period of unusual noises or vibrations - or just something different in how the car responds. Being very aware of the sound and feel of your car can prevent sudden danger and damage.

2.6.10 Distractions

> <u>Key points:</u> - Directing your attention includes deciding where
> it should <u>not</u> be.
>
> - Notice when people around you are distracted,
> because they are likely to be a threat.

We said before that a distraction is:

anything that takes your attention away from where it is needed.

This is the exact opposite of concentration. How high would you expect the average level of actual driver attention to be?

It is generally estimated to be about 20%. So most drivers have a strong assumption that "nothing will go wrong". And this in itself creates danger that will be significant in the casualty figures.

Driver inattention has been cited as:

the biggest cause of crashes,

above the more popular culprits like speed, alcohol and tailgating.

With our focus here being on the thinking side of driving, this is not a surprise. A large volume of research all confirms the catastrophic effect on safety. Unfortunately, not much of it sees the light of day, and lack of attention escapes the spotlight that it deserves.

Furthermore, "attention" cannot be measured out on the road, or by a crash investigator after an incident. So it rarely shoulders its share of the blame for the carnage. Certainly, drivers would not admit to crashing through not paying attention - even perhaps to themselves. Something else is blamed, and the real problem survives.

Young drivers are very prone to distractions, especially from their mates in the car, and this contributes to their poor record. Also, of course, when two distracted drivers meet, the danger skyrockets.

*Deciding where your attention <u>should be</u> includes
knowing where it should <u>not</u> be.*

To most people, their alertness is about "looking", but our fabulous gift of free will creates different types of distraction:

- Of the mind

    Any part, or even all, of your thinking can be diverted.

    It might start in observation, but then will also run right through into risk assessment and deciding actions.

    This is probably the most dangerous distraction.
    Keeping the brain engaged is absolutely vital, since the eyes and hands will usually follow.

- Of the eyes

    Even this is about more than looking.

    It prevents the whole observation chain of looking-seeing-understanding from even starting.

- Of the hands

    Leaves you less able to take action when needed.

    Normally, the most critical thing is being able to steer accurately, exactly when required.

You may, of course, be distracted in all of these ways at once, such as by a mobile phone.

Underestimating the threat of distractions can come from over-concentration on the physical side of driving. Since in normal driving, simply operating the machine is not demanding, and allows a feeling that little attention is needed.

There is also a clear link between being prone to distractions and having poor judgement of risk, because:

> being oblivious to the dangers
> encourages the mind to find something else to do.

However, there is another reason why this topic is here in the observation chapter, and it is rarely considered. How often do you:

> notice when the <u>other</u> road users around you are distracted?

This is a tremendously powerful observation, especially in helping you to predict when someone else is likely to make an error.

So there is a dual purpose in understanding distractions. Firstly and most obviously, to avoid them yourself. But then also to become better at spotting when other road users are distracted too.

> Anyone around you who is distracted is a real threat.

We can divide distractions into four sources:

1. Something outside the car

An object or event takes your attention, but does not pose a threat to you.

It might be a shop window display, a friend across the street, a breathtaking landscape, the scene of a crash, and so on.

2. Something inside the car

Most commonly this is passengers, especially children, doing things that take your attention.

It might be as simple as talking to you. Or perhaps starting to get a bit more actively bored in the back. If you carry a loose pet, that may also be a source of danger.

3. Driver activities

These include using the non-essential controls at the wrong time, such as heating, windows, sound system, navigation system, etc.

Then also "personal needs", such as using the phone, smoking, eating and drinking, map-reading, reading books or newspapers, studying work papers, shaving, applying make-up, etc.

The things that drivers get up to are sometimes quite bizarre.

You will have seen many, especially on the major roads when drivers have "settled in" to their driving.

A remarkably pointless, yet common, practice is for a driver to turn and look directly at their passenger when talking to them. Is it really more important to look at the passenger than the road?

Smoking can reduce steering control due to the hand distraction. And even more alarming is when live ash drops into a driver's lap!

Looking to the future, navigation and information systems are raising concerns about the level of distraction that is being placed directly into the cockpit.

4. Competing thoughts

This may be an "active" distraction by having definite worries on your mind. They may be to do with work, money, relationships, etc. Or it may be "passive", which is being caught up in:

a daydream through being not really engaged with the task.

Especially interesting is the mobile phone phenomenon. The surge in using a phone in the car is largely a symptom of how much "spare" attention drivers think they have.

But when the legislation, at the end of 2003, just banned <u>holding</u> the phone, it missed the point. It left the stronger distraction of the mind in place, and could even be seen as condoning having the call, as long as it is hands-free.

Even less understood is that the language task can be preferred by the brain, which then actively suppresses the visual-spatial ability that is essential to driving.

Have you ever wondered why people on the phone look as if they are in a daze?

Of course, it is impossible to legislate distraction out of driving - or anything else. We already know that:

the mind will always go to whatever it finds interesting.

It can be attracted, but not forced. And this is why making a task more engaging can be so effective in achieving a more natural concentration and avoiding distractions.

And that is precisely why one of the aims throughout this book is to make your driving more involving. It cannot fail to have a dramatic effect on your level of attention.

But here are some additional and specific ways that you can deal with distractions:

- **Set the priority**

  Consciously decide that whenever you get into the car:

  the driving task will take priority over everything else.

  Give yourself at least that much of a chance!

- **Remove conflicts**

  Avoid <u>planning</u> to do things while driving. Whether it is work, having a meal, adjusting something that could be done before you set off, or anything else.

- **Assess passengers**

  Know what to expect from them - especially young children. Give your own children good car habits right from the beginning!

- **Stop if necessary**

  Be prepared to stop safely to do something if it would otherwise be dangerous.

- **Avoid the delusion**

  Do not fall into the trap of thinking that driving skill is proved by the number of other things you can do at the same time!

- **Choose your moment**

  Before doing anything away from the core task:

  decide carefully when you do it.

  Wait for a time when risk is low, and you can spare some attention safely. Avoid, for example, choosing to change the CD when approaching a roundabout, or continuing a conversation through a very busy junction.

Vitally, understand that most distractions are things that drivers <u>choose</u> to do. And research confirms, unsurprisingly, that most crashes and near-misses are preceded by the driver being distracted.

Above all, remember that being aware of distractions has a dual purpose. Keeping your own attention level high is only the beginning.

After that, you should also:

notice and protect yourself against anyone else who is distracted.

You might be quite alarmed as you begin to realise how low the attention level is in some of the people around you.

Skill 7: Risk assessment and control

> **Key points:** - Safety is about properly balancing together **all** of the causes of risk.
>
> - **No single cause of danger holds the answer to your driving being safe.**

The purpose of this skill is to help you assess and control the dangers that your observation has identified. If there is one skill that had to be chosen as the most vital, this would be it. There are more pages in this chapter than any other.

As we saw in the Driving Process, this is where you make your judgements about danger, and also:

decide on your intentions and what actions to take.

Recall that this skill is closely coupled with your Observation. Brilliant observation is sterile if your risk handling is weak, and vice versa. Indeed, this section will help you to understand just <u>why</u> certain things are so critical to observe.

We explored what risk is before, and how vital it is to identify those risks that need to be dealt with. If you have not already done so, you should read the Sense of Danger skill, which explains that there are three factors involved in the probability of a collision:

1. **Speed**
2. **Surprise**
3. **Space**

And these were written as a simple model for the <u>probability</u> of a crash occurring, showing that more Speed or Surprise tend to increase risk, whereas more Space tends to decrease it:

$$\text{Risk} = \frac{\text{Speed} \times \text{Surprise}}{\text{Space}}$$

Avoiding collisions is achieved by:

balancing all three together in every situation.

No single factor can be isolated as "the magic answer" to danger. And even more, over-concentration on one point is likely to create weakness elsewhere across your full set of interlocking skills.

Next, the <u>consequences</u> of a potential crash should set the safety margin you want in preventing it from happening. And this involves a further two factors:

1. **What** you would hit   - and how easily the objects would be damaged.
2. **How hard**   - and the forces inflicted by the speed of impact.

Notice that all five of these factors are things that your <u>observation can detect</u>.

A deep and intuitive "feel" for risk can be built around this simple structure. And this in turn will develop the strong instincts that will help to keep you out of trouble.

2.7.1 Speed

<u>Key points</u>: - **Your assessment of the risks in your speed should be very objective.**

- **And controlling speed is not an isolated element of safety.**

We noted earlier that opinions on speed have become very polarised. And these strikingly different views, that are held for different reasons, have become a tangle of emotions too.

But irrespective of the rights or wrongs of each side, this situation is unhelpful for road safety.

And the highly charged nature of the subject makes it even more vital to explore it carefully.

Indeed, you can only properly assess and control the real risk in your speed by being objective.

Recall the position of Speed in the model:

$$\text{Risk} \ = \ \frac{\text{Speed} \ \text{x} \ \ \text{Surprise}}{\text{Space}}$$

In the quest for a negligible risk of collision, the vital question here is:

**"How well can I change speed or direction
to avoid a potential collision?"**

As your speed increases, so does your committed motion. This is the basic physics of momentum. And your job is to understand how much of a threat this carries.

But clearly, the speed of others on the road is also crucial in your decisions. And there is:

a wide range of behaviours for you to cope with.

Some drivers are constantly in a rush, and try not to slow for anything. They berate the incompetence of anyone in their way. Whereas others are habitually slow, and fail to see when it is safe to go more quickly. These drivers are convinced that anyone who passes them is reckless. And there are many others in between - thus the potential for abrasion as we all share the same roads.

Significantly, in nature's terms, humans are the only creature to harness a mechanical contrivance to go so fast. From the bicycle to the airplane, we regularly exceed our biological design speed.

And the benefits are stunning throughout the modern world. But the artificial power coupled with our still fragile bodies means that speed must be used with care.

Interestingly, surveys of driver pet hates show that people who go too slowly and obstruct traffic flow are a bigger annoyance than those who go too fast.

It is also true that:

taking speed in isolation is an increasingly common mistake.

So never forget that speed is just one of the things you control, and must fit in with everything else that is happening.

2.7.1.1 Legal speeding

> **Key points:**   - **Choosing a safe speed is your own responsibility, and cannot be delegated to a speed limit.**
>
>   - **More casualties happen in crashes that are below speed limits than above them.**

Let's start the topic of speed right in the tiger's mouth - with speeding. This is a high focus subject by any measure! The thing to avoid, though, is that speed limits occupy so much of your thinking as to take your mind off the full breadth of skills you need to use. No one wants that to happen.

It would certainly be a cruel deceit to suggest that sticking to speed limits is the main safety obligation that a driver has. Or indeed that driving slowly is automatically safe.

Your attention to risk must be infinitely more rigorous than that.

The immovable point is that:

choosing a safe speed is your own responsibility.
You cannot delegate it to a speed limit - or to anything else.

Even more, no one should dispute that choosing a safe speed in real situations must depend on a lot of variable things. And the Sense of Danger model has given us a solid framework for what they are. So it is wishing for the impossible to expect a speed limit to define the boundary of safety for you.

And then, following this through:

> although the law gives us one definition of speeding,
> it is better to think of <u>two</u>.

These two forms of speeding are:

1. **Exceeding the posted limit** - this is illegal, and the basis of the "speeding" offence that is prosecuted in law. It is purely numerical, easy to measure, and may be unsafe.

2. **Too fast for the situation** - but within the speed limit. By definition, this is <u>always</u> dangerous, though not illegal as a speed in itself - thus the term "legal speeding". It depends on the situation, and is a judgement that instruments cannot measure.

The first of these is usually called "excessive" speed, and the second "inappropriate" speed (though not always consistently).

However, although the word "inappropriate" sounds more innocent than "excessive", it is in fact far more guilty in terms of carnage. More casualties happen at legal speeds than illegal ones. And confusion over the relationship between speed and danger is one of the most treacherous elements in our driving culture.

It leads, for example, to claims like, "It wasn't dangerous, I wasn't speeding" - which is a nonsense. Or even the television campaign in which a young girl pleads to be hit at 30mph rather than 40mph - to improve her chances of survival.

The mistake is that the higher chance of survival almost implies that 30mph is an "acceptable", or even blameless, speed to hit the child!

It is vital that both the <u>legal</u> and the <u>safety</u> aspects are worked together into your speed decisions. The first is sign-posted on the road, but:

> the second part you need to decide for yourself.

And you must guard against the "illusion of safety" in simply travelling at a speed limit.

Critically, you must judge when <u>any</u> speed is too fast - especially below the limit when you might also be tempted to believe that the law gives you permission. A legal speed does not mean it is safe. However, round the other way, when you judge that travelling above the speed limit would be safe, then the law overrides taking the opportunity.

So the challenge here is to improve your skill in understanding and judging the actual danger of speed. Driving legally is fundamental, but don't imagine that sticking to a numeric speed limit is a skill - it is simply obeying the law. The actual skill is in assessing and controlling real danger, and:

> being able to make balanced decisions about what to do - at any speed.

2.7.1.2 Seven deceptions of speed

> **Key points**: - **Speed can deceive you in many different ways.**
> - **And you should know them all.**

As you drive along, constantly trying to gauge the implications of your speed, there are specific deceptions that interfere with that process.

Certainly, when so many drivers do things like following just as closely at 70mph as they do at 30mph, it suggests there is:

> something that confuses what their speed should be telling them.

These deceptions include:

1. **Speed perception**

   This is probably more subjective than you realise.

   - **Visual sense**

     You learned at school that speed is relative - depending on what is taken as the stationary point. And your perception works in the same way, so is easily fooled by looking at something moving.

     If your gaze is fixed on the traffic in front, for example, part of your perception will signal that you are hardly moving at all. This is why drivers feel so comfortable to bunch up in thick traffic, even when it is fast.

     It works by confusing actual speed with relative speed. In fact, if you push really tight up behind something big:

     > you can lose your visual sense of motion almost entirely.

     A similar effect occurs in poor visibility or at night, when it is harder to get a fix on the scenery.

   - **Physical motion sense**

     For decades, engineers have been designing the mechanical realities out of our cars, making them more like sitting in the lounge at home. Cosy seats, sound insulation, smooth suspension, low vibration, warm environment, your favourite music playing...

     All of this deprives your senses and creates a sort of virtual reality, with a feeling that nothing important is happening.

   - **Familiarity**

     The brain comes to accept any constant speed as "normal" after a while, and worthy of little attention. This can be seen when you slow down quickly from high speed, perhaps from motorway cruising speed into a junction roundabout. For a while it seems that you have almost stopped, with your sense of movement numbed.

2. Braking distance

As speed rises, the distance that your brakes need to stop you stretches out by more than you would naturally expect.

It lengthens with the square of the speed (see Maximum Braking later in this chapter), and again this might be reminiscent of school days - this time "kinetic energy", which increases in the same way. So doubling your speed quadruples your braking distance, and three times the speed takes nine times the distance, and so on.

This makes it much easier to misjudge braking hard from high speed. Especially since it is not something that drivers practise. So if you are forced into emergency braking, your car's behaviour may come as quite a shock. And:

*when braking in the wet, this deception is
even more dramatic!*

3. Damage potential

The braking effect above is a sign that there can be far more raw energy locked up in motion than we realise.

Speed comes so easily, with just a quiet squeeze on an eager throttle. And is tamed again with gentle pressure on powerful brakes. You rarely need to comprehend how much power the engine puts into the car, or the brakes absorb back out. In the absence of a drama it all stays discreetly hidden under the sleek bodywork.

So you probably never imagined that at 70mph a car has enough momentum to soar 50 metres vertically into the air. This is the height of a 15 storey block of flats!

Or from just 30mph you could jump the average house.

The spectacular stunts in movies are usually done at quite low speed, despite the flying effects.

In a crash, the impact has all this concealed energy to absorb - and in a split second. Thus the punishing outcome of fast impacts.

4. Journey times

Going faster saves some time, by definition. But the gains you expect can be elusive. So much of modern traffic is governed by congestion or speed limits, that:

*the opportunities to press on may exist for
only short parts of a journey.*

Even on long drives across the country the difference between a "relaxed" and "urgent" style is likely to be far less than you might hope for - perhaps only 5-10% of the total time. Paying good attention at junctions will often save more time by avoiding unnecessary setbacks.

5. Alertness

Concentration tends to drift lower when drivers have to settle for travelling slower than they naturally want to go. Again, this might be due to a speed limit or prolonged congestion, but:

the slower task seems to be far less demanding.

It can happen anywhere, from town to motorway, but you should expect a pull into a more lethargic style.

The likely effects include: poor observation, slow reactions, close following and being more easily distracted.

A conscious effort is needed to stay focused on the dangers that are still there. Plus, of course, you should expect that:

the drivers around you will suffer the same influence too.

In fact, it is much more vital for safety to stay alert to the road than to closely watch your speed. The un-alert driver can easily lose 2-3 seconds in reaction time, whereas a vigilant driver could shed 40-60mph of speed in that time if necessary.

6. Accelerating to safety

Some people insist that drivers can never accelerate out of trouble, and that increasing speed cannot make a situation safer. But, in reality, it depends on how bad you let the trouble become!

If the danger is allowed to escalate until a collision is quite likely, then resolving it with acceleration may not be possible.

Usually by this stage the threatening impact will be directly in front of you. And even if it is at the side or behind, acceleration may be too weak to escape.

However, your primary aim is to keep risk far below this level. And in doing this, it is wrong to assume that braking is the only response to an emerging hazard. Instead, you should expect to find that some early risks can be diffused more effectively by moving forward than by pulling back.

Without doubt, expert drivers will:

use both acceleration and deceleration to
adjust their position in traffic,

and to keep risk low - especially in multi-lane flows or driving through junctions. Both pedals are there to be used - with equal care.

Paradoxically, this can be even more true in congested traffic, where braking can easily increase risk by disrupting a steady flow. Of course, before accelerating you do need a safe space in front of you to use! And one of the very good reasons for not tailgating is to create this extra option.

Consider some examples:

- imagine you are the blue car in this dual carriageway scene, with a strong threat from the volume of joining traffic. What should you do?

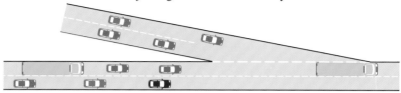

The best option is to accelerate into the empty space ahead of you. This takes you out of the impending squeeze, and releases more space for the others too. Doing nothing is reckless, and braking would make matters worse by compacting the flow behind even more into the point of merging.

- in another case, the green car is gaining on the truck in front, and indicates to ask for a space to pass.

Again, the best option for the blue car is to move decisively forward and let him out behind, rather than brake and cause a shock wave back up the line. Doing nothing will force the green car to brake hard as he runs out of space in his own lane - or he will lunge out anyway and force your violent reaction.

Much better still if you had seen earlier the situation the green car was getting into, and adjusted your position to avoid becoming part of the problem.

7. Rule-dependence

The most recognised rule on speed is in the Highway Code:

> "Drive at a speed that will allow you to stop well within the distance you can see to be clear. ...The safe rule is never to get closer than the overall stopping distance."

It sounds sensible enough, but the idea that your safe speed can be decided by a rule is fatally flawed. In practice, situations and hazards are too complex, and there is no substitute for your own good judgement. So never forget that a rule cannot set a safe speed for you, and it is a reckless deception to expect that it can.

There are also other dangers wrapped up in this rule that make it controversial, and these are explained in the next section.

Even more though, it is certainly true that most experienced drivers rarely need to consult their speedometer except to stay legal. And it is interesting to wonder what would happen if your speedometer stopped working. Would you suddenly start having crashes, or might it instead raise your alertness to the dangers you face...?

It will be clear, though maybe a little confusing, that these deceptions pull in different directions. Such is life, and this simply makes it important to:

be aware of them all - not just some of them.

2.7.1.3 The Golden Rule

> **Key point**: - No rule can replace using your own good judgement to decide a safe speed.

This follows on from the last section, which closed on the most widely recognised "golden rule" for safe speed, that is in the Highway Code:

> "Drive at a speed that will allow you to stop well within the distance you can see to be clear...
>
> The safe rule is never to get closer than the overall stopping distance...
>
> Allow at least a two-second gap between you and the vehicle in front on roads carrying fast traffic."

We can draw a number of valuable points from how this rule is used that will help your judgement.

The last section showed the concern about letting any rule set your speed and distance. But there are also specific dangers in this rule that you need to take into account:

- it invites head-on crashes
- it implies that an empty space is a safe one
- it seems to condone driving on the limit of maximum braking
- the "stopping distance" rule conflicts with the "two-second gap".

Let's take them in turn.

Head-on crashes

Devastating crashes are invited where two vehicles drive towards each other and need the same space in which to stop, such as on narrow country roads.

This concerns the passage: "... well within the distance you can see to be clear".

In practice, the word "well" is forgotten as people recall this rule, and it is taken to mean using the stopping distances in the table.

And this seems to be confirmed by:

"The safe rule is never to get closer than the overall stopping distance".

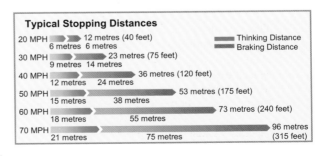

Typical Stopping Distances

- Thinking Distance
- Braking Distance

20 MPH — 12 metres (40 feet)
6 metres   6 metres

30 MPH — 23 metres (75 feet)
9 metres   14 metres

40 MPH — 36 metres (120 feet)
12 metres   24 metres

50 MPH — 53 metres (175 feet)
15 metres   38 metres

60 MPH — 73 metres (240 feet)
18 metres   55 metres

70 MPH — 96 metres (315 feet)
21 metres   75 metres

Imagine you are driving out in the country, on a fine summer day. The road is good, and the rule allows you to drive up to the 60mph limit. A slight bend comes up and the road narrows slightly to single track. But you can still see that 240 feet ahead is clear, which is the stopping distance shown for 60mph (60 feet thinking, plus 180 feet braking), so you press on. If you meet a stationary object, you can stop in time.

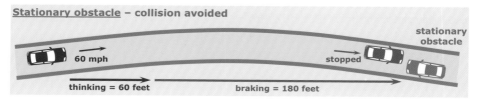

Stationary obstacle – collision avoided

Then, around the bend you meet your motoring twin coming the other way - obeying the same rule, at the same speed. But now you are each looking at the <u>same</u> piece of road as your stopping distance. Using the Highway Code figures, you would crash head-on while both doing 49mph! Which would be difficult to survive...

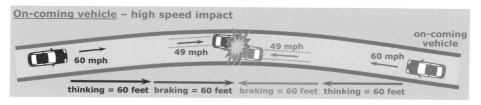

On-coming vehicle – high speed impact

It is a dramatic case, but the lesson is crystal clear. The rule fails when two approaching vehicles need the same space to stop. In ordinary situations it allows awesome collisions.

In truth, though, every advanced or expert driver reading this scenario will have thought it insane. The words "...and the road narrows..." will have triggered an instant braking response, and after that the events became unreal. They would:

instinctively override the rule and slow down.

Still using the Highway Code figures, the maximum speed at which the cars can enter this bend is 40mph - assuming they can both do superb emergency stops. This would feel very much slower than 60mph. And if one is faster, the other must be slower.

You may see the problem as obvious. The possibility of <u>oncoming</u> traffic changes everything. Which is clearly true. It is far more threatening than something stationary. However, similarly then, is it <u>less</u> threatening to follow a vehicle going in the <u>same</u> direction? The answer depends on the wider situation, of course.

But:

if the rule is based on meeting static objects,

it is vital to recognise the limitation - especially for the case of oncoming traffic.

Empty space

In the passage: *"...the distance you can see to be clear"*, the common understanding of "clear" is "empty" - nothing in the way.

The example above showed that you cannot treat the road ahead as clear if something can come towards you into the space you need for yourself. But the trap is bigger than that, because a vehicle, cyclist or pedestrian, can enter your "clear" path <u>from the side</u> even more quickly, and the rule will not help you at all.

Picture yourself driving along a straight "empty" road. There is a car in a side street waiting to come out.

It is stationary, but the driver is looking the other way, not at you. Is your road "clear"?

Now the driver looks at you. So what difference does that make?

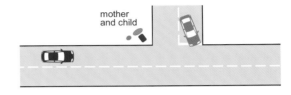

mother and child

But in the same moment the mother waiting to cross on the corner has let go of her child's hand to move the pushchair... Do you plough on regardless?

There are many threats to an empty space that should change whether you treat it as "clear". And your speed decisions must weigh them all into the balance.

Limit of braking

Now come again to the piece:

"The safe rule is never to get closer than the overall stopping distance",

and the table that comes with it.

Unfortunately, the rule and the table together suggest quite clearly that it is safe to drive on the limit of maximum braking ability.

Which is definitely not true!

The risk level is far too high. And it sets you up for frequent harsh braking, and a crash if ever you get it slightly wrong.

Typical Stopping Distances

20 MPH	12 metres (40 feet)	▬ Thinking Distance
	6 metres 6 metres	▬ Braking Distance
30 MPH	23 metres (75 feet)	
	9 metres 14 metres	
40 MPH	36 metres (120 feet)	
	12 metres 24 metres	
50 MPH	53 metres (175 feet)	
	15 metres 38 metres	
60 MPH	73 metres (240 feet)	
	18 metres 55 metres	
70 MPH	96 metres (315 feet)	
	21 metres 75 metres	

In addition, of course, such braking would create havoc for the traffic around you, and the high probability of getting belted from behind.

Perhaps this helps a little to explain why rear shunts are the most popular type of crash!

Conflicting advice

Two measures are used in this rule.

The first is <u>distances</u>: "...never to get closer than the overall stopping distance".

And the other is <u>time</u>: "Allow at least a two-second gap...". Although, the "at least" part is largely overlooked.

Indeed, the stunningly successful publicity campaign taught us to measure the time exactly, with the unforgettable chant, "Only a fool breaks the 2-second rule".

But which should you use - the distances or 2 seconds? And are they the same, being together in the same rule?

In fact, they are very different, coinciding at only one speed - which calculates out to be 19mph. This is the speed from which it takes 2 seconds to stop (on Highway Code figures, including thinking time). Above this, the time increases far beyond that figure.

From 70mph it takes an eternal 5.5 seconds to stop,

and after 2 seconds you are still doing 51mph! (See also Stopping Ability next).

You may think this is all right, being confident you can stop as quickly as the chap in front. But this assumes they do not hit something that stops them quicker. And this is exactly the mechanism that unleashes multiple pile-ups!

So now, do you need a rule that takes account of the gap in front of the car you are following? Plus the gaps further up the line too? And the gap behind is also important, since it is cold solace to miss the car in front if the one behind ploughs into you anyway.

Many changes have been suggested to this Highway Code rule over the years. All of them have been aimed at resolving one or more of the problems in:

- head-on crashes
- clear space
- maximum braking

But the safest conclusion, when deciding your safe speed and distance is:

do not look to trust your life to a rule.

Nothing can replace your own assessment of the total actual situation. Every threat around you must be part of your decisions, and it is treacherous to expect a <u>rule</u> to do this for you.

On the question of whether distance or time is a better gauge of braking risk - this is covered in Maximum Braking, later in this chapter.

2.7.1.4 Stopping ability

> **Key point:** - **It is better to rehearse emergency braking than meet a crisis unprepared.**

We saw before, that drivers generally have little idea of how quickly their car can stop - or more crucially will <u>not</u> stop. It is especially true at high speed, or in the wet.

Fortunately, severe crises are rare events. But this does mean that drivers are ill-prepared to do very hard braking if it does become necessary.

And yet, it is undeniable that:

> **most major crashes include a failed emergency stop!**

However, the seeds of the problem are sown at a very early stage. During L-test tuition emergency stops are done at 30mph or less, in dry conditions and after a warning from the instructor. The car stops almost instantaneously, and is <u>very</u> easy to control. Even more, since 1999, an emergency stop is no longer asked for in most tests. This allows novices to believe that the ability to brake "hard and safely" is not important. And, anyway, they have done it as well as is necessary.

Clearly, it is better to avoid the need for heavy braking altogether, but the risk is magnified by having to take action in a crisis that is so unfamiliar. The chances of getting the best outcome are low, and:

> **crashes will occur simply because emergencies are badly handled.**

In other areas crises are thoroughly rehearsed. Offices have fire drills, hospitals practise their response to major incidents, and so on. Yet drivers rely on raw "panic reactions", which is exactly the wrong thing to do. Some drivers even refuse to practise heavy braking, having heard that the ABS will "feel funny"! This can be a killer, because people who feel ABS in action for the first time often release the pressure, thinking that something has broken.

Practising heavy braking is best done at off-road training events that cover extreme manoeuvres. They are highly focused and enlightening sessions, and are run to be enjoyable too. Drivers gain a good practical feel for their car's capability - and crucially, its limitations too. This type of training is popular with company car drivers. Only practise any braking on the roads if you can find opportunities you are certain are <u>absolutely</u> safe.

Certainly, there is little point in having powerful brakes if:

> **the car could handle a crisis, but the driver cannot make it do so.**

Stopping distance

Stopping distance is usually seen as having two parts, though there is often a third element too:

1. Thinking time

This is the time it takes to react. That is, to perceive the danger, decide to brake, and get your foot to the pedal.

The Highway Code figures assume you do all of that in about two-thirds of a second. It is a constant time for all speeds, though the distance covered varies, of course. But this is quick, and looks like an "ideal" case.

In practice, it is lengthened by a variety of things, such as: low alertness, poor observation, a specific distraction, tiredness, alcohol, drugs, and even emotional state.

This means that, in real situations, with an unsuspecting driver, response times can easily rise to:

two seconds or more.

Disastrous though that sounds.

The most crucial point, though, is what you are reacting to - and whether it is the car in front, or the wider situation you can see developing further ahead.

2. Braking distance

This is the distance covered while the brakes are on. In theory, this increases with the square of speed, as we said before, but there are other factors too, such as:

- **vehicle**: differences in the type of vehicle, braking system and tyres all affect braking performance. Especially, those without modern brakes or with heavy loads will need much longer to stop.

- **road**: any surface that is not dry and firm will reduce braking efficiency to some degree. Travelling up or down an incline will also make a difference. Special high-grip surfaces, that are laid at trouble spots, are effective at improving braking.

- **driver**: the capability of the machine may or may not be used well. This one is totally down to you.

Of major effect, though, are:

the advances in braking systems over the years.

Braking is now highly power assisted, with discs that are more effective than drums, and has electronic controls such as ABS. Better suspension, tyres and road surfaces have helped too.

As a result, most modern cars have braking distances that are about 30% less than the Highway Code table, which is a huge difference.

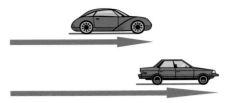

The table was first published over five decades ago, of course, in the days of much cruder machinery.

However, the origin of the Highway Code figures is largely academic in the sense that few people commit the distances to memory anyway. And their usefulness is also limited because our judgement of measured distance is quite poor (ie the number of metres or feet). More practically:

**we use the "feel" of the car in action to gauge
how well we expect it to stop.**

You should also be alert to the wide range of braking abilities in the traffic that surrounds you. Especially the vehicles directly in front and behind. Generally, older cars have worse braking. But much more alarmingly:

large trucks can need up to three times as long to stop as a car,

because of their weight and brake design. Yes, <u>three</u> times! Beware also, that motorbikes lose stability easily, having only two wheels. Plus, of course, there are inevitable variations in driver alertness that will affect how quickly they can stop.

3. Brake light delay

This is the third element, though it comes first in the sequence. It is relevant when you are reacting to the brake lights in front.

Standard bulbs take about a <u>fifth of a second</u> to light up after the switch has been closed by the pedal.

If that sounds insignificant, notice that at 70mph this is an extra 6 metres of travel before you get the chance to even begin thinking what is happening.

And under maximum braking:

this fraction of time is equal to about 4mph of your speed.

It is constant as we will see later, so you could go from 70 to 66mph, or 35 to 31mph, and so on. This would definitely soften an impact, and might even prevent some too.

Tailgating convoys are especially prone to this effect as the lost time accumulates whenever a braking wave shoots down the line.

Help is on the way, though, with a new type of light that uses Light Emitting Diodes (LEDs) that have no delay. They will remove this element of the braking sequence as soon as they can be phased into common use.

2.7.1.5 Maximum braking - another view

> **Key points:**
> - **Stopping ability is easier to judge as time than as a distance.**
> - **It is not rational to drive on the limit of maximum braking - half that level is a better standard.**

Braking performance is normally expressed in distance - the number of metres to stop from a certain speed (on a good, dry surface). But it can also be measured in time - the number of seconds to come to rest.

As we saw before, the table in the Highway Code uses distances, though the rule also introduces the idea of using time:

- "...never get closer than the overall stopping distance"
- "Allow at least a two-second gap..."

So the question when you are judging risk is:

which is it more meaningful to use, distance or time?

And the answer is likely to be <u>time</u> - for two reasons:

1. Time is easier to judge

People find it quite tricky to gauge measured distances, especially when moving. And it is not easy to improve the ability either. Whereas for time, the famous chant, "Only a fool breaks the 2-second rule", showed us a simple way to count in seconds.

It can be extended by adding, "...or the 3-second rule, or the 4-second rule..." etc. Or there are other chants that will do just as well, including simply learning to count in seconds, "none...one...two...", but don't forget to start at "none", not "one"!

You can practise the pace against the rhythm of a loud clock or the second-hand of your watch, and acceptable accuracy should come fairly quickly. This little skill is also useful in measuring other elements of risk too - see Driving Plans later, under Surprise.

2. The time relationship is simpler

Braking <u>distance</u> increases with speed on an exponential curve, which can be difficult to gauge, but:

braking <u>time</u> increases with speed on a <u>straight line</u>,

which is therefore much easier for the brain to handle!

Here are the graphs for distance and time. They each show the maximum braking lines for Highway Code (HC) figures and the modern car average (sales over the past 10 years):

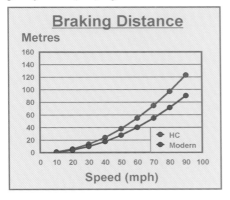

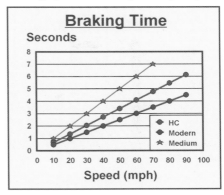

For the metres scale:
- distance rises on a curve (with the square of speed)
- drivers forget the figures
- absolute distances are hard to judge, especially on the move

For the seconds scale:
- time rises with speed on nice straight lines
- these are much simpler to understand and use
- we already count in seconds for the 2-second rule

The graph for time also shows another line - the top one, which is for medium braking in modern cars. Because driving on the limit of maximum braking is not sensible:

this "medium" level is set at <u>half</u> the emergency level.

This is quite firm, but calm and easy to control. It is a much more practical standard to use in normal driving. And it builds in a useful safety margin.

By a quirk of mathematical chance, the braking <u>times</u> have very memorable relationships with speed (still on a good, dry surface):

Braking time		30mph	60mph
Highway Code:	$\dfrac{mph}{15}$ seconds	2 secs	4 secs
Modern cars:	$\dfrac{mph}{20}$ seconds	1.5 secs	3 secs
Medium braking:	$\dfrac{mph}{10}$ seconds	3 secs	6 secs

Dividing by 10 for medium braking (or by 20 for maximum braking) is very easy to remember. Don't forget, though, that this is only the braking time. Thinking time must be added too - which will be about 1 second if you are very alert, or longer if you are not.

Therefore, if you decide to adopt a style that should need no more than medium braking, your yardstick, with 1 second alert thinking time, becomes simply:

$$\text{Stopping time} = \frac{\text{mph}}{10} + 1 \;\; \text{seconds}$$

This is 7 seconds at 60mph, and 4 seconds at 30mph, etc. And contrasted with the 2-second rule, this may change your thinking a little...

But don't take any of this as a rule. It is simply information to help you balance the risks in all your various situations. The crucial point is to show the margin of safety you have on braking. And especially how to avoid it being negative!

Certainly, whenever you adopt a short following position, it is clearer now just <u>how dependent</u> you are on being fully alert and anticipating well beyond the vehicle in front.

Again, the idea of "medium" braking is introduced specifically to move away from the notion of driving on the limit of maximum braking. Relying on severe braking to meet trouble is to routinely carry very high risk - which will eventually catch you out. Whereas:

a driving style that needs only light braking is
a sign of using some high calibre skills.

2.7.1.6 Grip and skidding

<u>Key points</u>: - **Friction has a hidden treachery at its limit.**

- **Skid prevention is a more realistic skill**
   than skid control.

Unless you are a good rally driver, skidding is an extreme loss of control, and probably one of your worst nightmares on the road.

You can only control where your car goes if the tyres have grip. Every force of acceleration, braking and steering is transmitted through the little "footprints of fate" where the rubber meets the road.

But a skid is more the <u>symptom</u> of lost control than its cause. In other words, you lose control of the <u>situation</u> first, and the skid is the result.

And this emphasises that, in most cases:

drivers cause skids, not roads.

Even the worst road surface is passive until the driver arrives.

Most people associate skids with simply going too fast - which is why this topic is here under Speed. But in truth, there is more to it than that.

Causing a skid

The basic physics is clear. Two surfaces will slide over each other when:

the demand for friction exceeds what is available from the contact.

So both sides of the equation play a part and need to be carefully understood.

Taking the demand first. This is determined by the driver, through the actions of acceleration, braking and steering. It can be excessive in any combination of:

- accelerating too hard   - causing wheel-spin
- braking too hard   - usually in panic mode
- steering too sharply   - for the speed of the car.

If you brake hard while already pulled tight into a bend, the two demands for grip add together, and reach the limit before either would on their own. It is worth noting too that:

cornering forces on a curve increase with the square of speed

(just as braking distances do). Twice the speed needs four times the traction to stay on course, etc. The weight of a vehicle and its load also adds to the demand for grip.

Turning then to the available friction, this is more complex but reveals the real character of skids. Available friction depends on:

- the road surface, and the extent to which it is not firm and dry
- your tyres, and their condition and air pressure
- your suspension, and how well it maintains the road contact.

Therefore, and obviously, skidding is more likely with a poor road surface, worn tyres, wrong pressures, or faulty suspension.

The most common threat to grip is water. It often falls from the sky, and is an excellent lubricant for rubber! Compared to dry roads, crashes on wet roads are twice as likely to involve a skid, and on snow or ice four times as likely.

Predictably, when assessing the grip that a road surface can provide:

drivers have far worse judgement in poor weather.

And skids that involve loss of sideways control are usually more dangerous than ones that are straight ahead - because there is normally less space there to absorb the error.

Whatever friction is available, though, it is always divided across three things:

- the demand from changing speed
- the demand from changing direction
- whatever is left over, unused and in reserve.

Look at these three scenarios of grip, and one of slip:

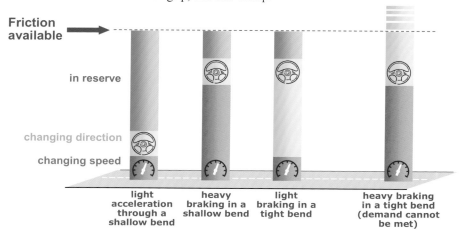

| light acceleration through a shallow bend | heavy braking in a shallow bend | light braking in a tight bend | heavy braking in a tight bend (demand cannot be met) |

But the threat in skids is deeper than just losing some grip. The crisis is compounded by a cruel twist in the way that friction behaves. And it explains why skids can be such spectacular events - especially in the wet or on ice.

Technically, it is that "dynamic" friction is less than "static" friction. Practically, it is that friction between <u>sliding</u> surfaces is less than when they were <u>gripping</u>. You might have experienced that pushing a heavy object across the floor is easier once the grip has been broken and it has started to slide.

The same occurs when tyres lose grip. But now your momentum pushes the skid on - for longer than you expected (or hoped!). Crucially, recovering traction is now more difficult, because:

> **the friction demand must fall a long way before the grip can return.**

This is why ABS works by pulsing the brakes on and off, rather than just easing them back slightly.

It is not easy to draw, but skids have three distinct phases:

1. increasing friction demand to the point of starting a skid
2. reducing friction demand to the point where grip returns
3. increasing friction demand again within the limit of grip.

These phases might be:

- braking ever harder, into a skid
- releasing most of the pressure
- and applying it again more gently.

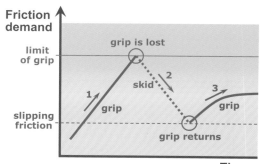

So this is the latent treachery of friction. It comes as a shock, because grip usually works so hard to keep us connected to the ground. But at the limit, it turns like the strike of a teased animal. And it is even more violent on wet or icy roads, because the grip is broken more completely than on a dry surface. This behaviour of friction is the real reason why major skids can start so dramatically, and then be difficult to stop.

Clearly, your best aim is to:

always have some grip confidently in reserve.

But there is still one last twist to the story. And it lies in what the <u>consequences</u> turn out to be. The problem is the sheer unpredictability of skids. The precise circumstances can dictate both good and bad fortune. A tiny sideways scuff in a busy bend could trigger a catastrophic head-on smash, while a massive slide on an uncrowded motorway might manage to escape any impact at all. You really can't tell, and:

sometimes it might take only a minor skid to spell disaster.

Skid control or prevention

Whether to control or prevent a skid has only one answer. No one should use public roads in a way that relies on being able to create and handle a skid. They are far too erratic.

However, skid training is definitely recommended. But you should be totally clear and realistic about which skills you will come away with to use on the roads - control or prevention.

The typical session on a skidpan can be deceptive. And in ways that match the Sense of Danger model:

- **Speed**

  Is very slow. The tyres are smooth and pumped rock hard, and the surface is soaked in oil and water. Slides then come easily and gently, at little more than walking pace.

- **Surprise**

  Is very low. You know the car will slide, and even induce it yourself. It is expected, and you are totally ready for it.

- **Space**

  Is comparatively vast, giving room to regain control. But even the gentle slides will equate to slewing across several lanes of highway, or plunging off into a ditch.

By the end of the day, if you are off-guard, these can:

lure you into an illusion of competence.

For practical reasons, the pace will have been sedate and the experience quite tame and non-threatening. There will have been no cause for panic, allowing your brain to maintain its own grip on what to do. In contrast, out on the real road, you will be going faster, not expect to slide, and have a very restricted space to use - and momentary panic will play its part too.

So why encourage drivers on to a skidpan? The reasons are better called to "gain skid experience" than to "learn skid control", that is to:

1. **Experience the slides**: directly feel how wayward the car is without good grip
2. **See the space**: discover for yourself how much space it takes to recover
3. **Learn avoidance**: feel what causes a skid, and how to reduce the risk
4. **Have some fun!**: vent some enthusiasm, and do some exciting things in a car in the right place for doing them!

You will certainly learn to control the skids that happen on a skidpan. But with the main focus on coming away with <u>prevention</u> skills, you can have a really good time - in a wide open space with only a few friendly cones to nudge over.

No attempt is made here to describe any of the techniques of skid control. It is even more tricky to do in a book than on the skidpan.

And there are also far too many variables to cope with, such as: the cause (braking, acceleration or steering), the surface (dry, wet, icy, loose), which end of the car breaks away first, which are the drive wheels (front, rear or all four), and so on.

Also confusing is that some of the corrective actions are naturally intuitive, but others are not - until you get the feel for them.

Of course, taking the wrong action can make the situation worse - like trying to catch a falling knife.

The vital point is that when skids happen with such suddenness:

the only skills available are the ones you regularly use,

and have kept well honed into instinctive reflexes. There will be no time for anything else - and this rules out skid control. Your main skill in skid <u>control</u> will be to work out afterwards what you should have done differently at the time.

Increasingly, electronic systems, such as ABS and Traction Control in various forms are installed in cars to intervene at the point of skidding. They can help, but cannot overcome the universal laws of motion, friction and momentum. And crucially, they stop being safety devices if they tempt drivers to push their car harder, and to lean on the technology for control.

Emphatically, on public roads:

skid <u>prevention</u> is the realistic driver skill,

coupled with being confident to handle your car within the limits of grip. Expert road drivers avoid skids, they don't rely on controlling them. They stay well connected to the road.

2.7.2 Surprise

> **Key point:** - When it is fully understood, surprise is probably the biggest source of danger on the road.

Sometimes we look forward to surprises, such as at Christmas, birthdays or other special occasions. These are the nice ones.

But on the road it is different, because:

collisions are caused by things we didn't expect to happen.

As a young driver confessed, trying to make light of it, "My girlfriend used to like surprises - till she saw my driving!".

Of all the threats out there, surprise is probably the biggest. If we could eradicate the unexpected, casualties would fall to zero (except for suicides). And there are very practical ways you can reduce surprise. Although you may hear "expect the unexpected" as a popular piece of advice, it is unfortunately an impossible cliché that simply begs the question of, "How?".

Reminding ourselves of the risk model again:

$$\text{Risk} = \frac{\text{Speed} \times \boxed{\text{Surprise}}}{\text{Space}}$$

This time the key measure is:

"How certain am I about what will happen next?"

Insurance companies see the word "suddenly" appearing time after time in accident report descriptions of the event just before the impact. Something happens that is too unexpected to handle.

Of course, you can never totally predict everything around you, so unexpected things occur all the time. Some are significant, while others are not, so you need to know clearly which are which. And then how to fix the ones that matter.

An important part of keeping risk low is to aim for a style in which everything you do is well planned and smoothly executed. But against that:

surprise causes rushed thinking and sudden actions.

And those actions are likely to be harsher than necessary too.

However, there is clearly a maximum level of action we are able to take.

For example, emergency braking and/or steering.

Above this, the surprise will result in collision even with the strongest action.

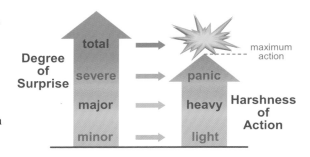

2.7.2.1 Defining surprise

> **Key point**:   - There are three types of surprise, and all are equally deadly.

Of the three factors of risk, Surprise is the least well understood. Speed and Space are both easy to grasp as very physical things, whereas Surprise is less tangible.

But every surprise holds a genuine potential for danger. Understanding this threat begins with knowing exactly what we mean by the term "surprise".

Our friendly dictionary tells us that surprise is "catching of persons unprepared". Unprepared! This is the crucial key, from which we can say that a surprise is:

> **"Anything you did not predict, that might need you to react".**

And within that, the most dangerous surprises are:

> **"Anything that makes you react before calmly checking it is safe".**

The first definition is broad and will show you the emerging risks early on, when adjusting to them is easier. The second highlights the situations you need the skills to avoid completely.

Most importantly, surprise robs you of the time you need to take decisions, and to act calmly and under control. When things happen suddenly they feel rushed - even perhaps a bit panicked. So surprise forces snap decisions and over-reactions, for example, severe braking for something in front, without even knowing what is behind.

Feeling rushed is a definite sign of danger.

Sometimes mere fractions of a second is enough to catch you wrong-footed. And even more time can be lost if the shock of a major surprise also throws you into a momentary paralysis.

Although big surprises are the most obvious, expert drivers are very rarely surprised at all. And they also don't do things that surprise other road users either - which is just as important.

It is useful to tackle surprise by seeing three types:

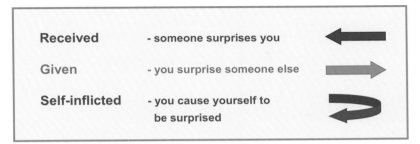

Received   - someone surprises you

Given   - you surprise someone else

Self-inflicted   - you cause yourself to be surprised

Up to now you might have only been thinking of the first one. But causing surprise to others is also dangerous to you. And you can surprise yourself by taking actions before thinking through the outcome. The following pages take each of these types in turn, under the titles:

- Anticipation
- Being predictable
- Driving plans.

Something to note about surprises is that they often cascade in a domino effect that rushes towards a collision. One surprise causes another, and so on. Typical are the braking waves in dense traffic that transmit a growing surprise down the line until it finds someone who can't handle it. Thus the importance of preventing the small ones.

A style that allows constant surprises also generates a lot of stress. You will be far more on edge when having to react to unexpected things. This resolves the apparent paradox that higher concentration makes driving a lot easier.

When things happen as expected, you are more easily in control.

So learning to reduce surprise in your driving should be a clear aim. It will gain you vital time that will dramatically lower risk and increase your calm control.

But as elsewhere, this will rest crucially on your honest self-assessment. If you deny your surprises as you find them, nothing will be gained. Indeed, you will probably blame others even more for things that go wrong. Instead, to gain expertise means you must seek out the opportunities to do so.

Paying attention to surprise is also a very powerful technique that will improve your observation. As we saw before:

the most potent measure of poor observation is the presence of surprise.

2.7.2.2 Anticipation - expect more

> **Key points**:
> - **You can't control events without first anticipating them.**
> - **Seeing the future starts with simply deciding to do it.**

How easily are you caught off guard - taken by surprise? Good anticipation will make you less vulnerable, and more self-reliant.

The specific aim is to predict threats. For every creature on the planet, knowing the immediate future is critical for survival, so nature makes a lot of brain power available for this activity. On the road, this instinct will help you project events forward and check for danger.

The big question is simply:

"What will happen next ?!?"

Your purpose, though, is not only to <u>know</u> what will happen, but to <u>influence</u> it by taking more control. It may be something as easy as adjusting speed to choose the moment you arrive into a tricky situation, so that it plays out differently. Entering a busy roundabout or merging traffic are simple examples.

Although anticipation relies on acute observation, it does not follow automatically from it. Noticing and understanding something is not the same as imagining what comes next. This is different thinking, and makes anticipation even more variable between people than observation is.

You may have heard the claim that, "Driving will always be dangerous, because you can't know what other people will do". This is the feeble excuse of a "determined victim", hoping to justify poor skill. You certainly can know what others are going to do - and often before they do themselves. Even more, it is often true that:

the "victim" in a crash is a "culprit" too in some measure,

by simply failing to see it coming.

But any anticipation needs specific attention. It can be easy to get so wrapped up in the present moment as to neglect the future. There is a phrase in aviation, "flying behind the plane", to describe a pilot who is so absorbed in what he is doing as to disregard what lies ahead. It applies to driving too, and:

your thinking must always be ahead of where you are.

There is another saying, "Never put your car where your eyes and brain have not been before".

How to see the future

If knowing something before it happens is so crucial, the vital question is "how to do it".

The answer starts in what you think about.

Fortunately, most things that road users do have a reason - even if it is a wrong one.

This gives you vital clues. And building good anticipation is largely about using as much evidence as you can find.

The future will reveal itself to you in many ways:

1. Decide to anticipate

- This may seem too obvious, but it is not. Many drivers don't even get to the stage of trying to predict, and it shows. So the key is to:

    put yourself into a state of "active expectation".

    Also, remember that predicting relies on acute observation, and expect that it may take some time to build a new habit of anticipating.

2. Look far ahead - as well as close to

- See the traffic patterns in the distance that show signs of danger. Perhaps thick merging traffic clogging a junction, or simply a patch of denser activity. Start assessing junctions as soon as they come into view. And look far behind for approaching faster vehicles - that may be hard to see, such as a nimble biker.

3. See events as a flow

- Most of what happens is in some way:

    a clear continuation of what is already taking place.

- You should not be caught off guard by the driver in front who is slow in reacting to cars up ahead that are stopping. Nor by the cyclist you can see in a side road who just continues to ride out into the traffic.

4. Understand causes

- The root cause of a threat is as important as its effect. If a cyclist could enter the path of an oncoming car, then that would determine what the car does next. And some risks can influence many road users at the same time. Someone misjudging an overtake will affect all the traffic in both directions.

- There may be specific situations that create uncertainty. For example, as road users react to the growing diversity of traffic calming obstacles, you should expect some unusual moves.

5. Understand other road users

- What are other people's intentions, and frustrations or distractions?

    What someone <u>wants</u> to do is a good sign of what they <u>will</u> do,

    and perhaps also the risks they may take too. A pedestrian may suddenly dart into the road - after spotting a friend. Or a car is likely to launch out of a junction - having waited for a very long time.

Also, you need to read their "road language" - subtle changes in position, direction and speed, as well as the formal signals. And beware if they are inconsistent - this will warn of actions that might otherwise seem totally impulsive.

- Where are they looking? Where someone looks will usually show you what they will do next. Beware of the exceptions though, like the driver so fascinated with something behind that they ignore what is in front. Or the pedestrian who steps off the footpath while looking backwards to say farewell to a friend.

- Could they change their mind? Sometimes people alter what they are doing quite abruptly - especially after showing signs of hesitation.

Have you ever seen a car going very slowly, that indicates to turn off, only to find it is the wrong street and go straight on - just as the car behind has started to pass?

Even more common is the car that starts to move on to a roundabout only to brake again suddenly. The answer is to always:

leave room for a change of mind, right up to their "point of no return".

6. Look for specific dangers

- How could someone else endanger you? Think about what they would have to do. This will focus your attention on the specific signs to watch for. A crucial point about people's mistakes is <u>when</u> you notice the possibility.

- Another very powerful predictor, especially of sudden moves, is to notice:

what dangers are other people in themselves?

Assessing someone else's risk is the same as knowing your own, but now you imagine yourself in their place.

7. Use stereotypes

- Road users often fit into a "type", especially those who create the danger. Recognising them will help you to expect what they do. (See Using Stereotypes in the next section.)

Be prepared, though, to see more than one possible outcome in your anticipation. Expectations are not certainties, and the aim is to be better prepared <u>whatever</u> happens.

Once you start to consciously anticipate it gets much easier - even quite addictive as it becomes more natural and intuitive. You will even begin to:

see what people will do before they know themselves,

because you have noticed why they will do it. At the expert level, anticipation can be almost like a psychic power!

2.7.2.3 Using stereotypes

> <u>Key points</u>:
> - **You already know more than you realise about the road users around you.**
> - **Using stereotypes will help you predict a lot more of what they will do.**
> - **What stereotype would <u>you</u> fit into...?**

This is about an effective technique to improve your anticipation. By using something simple that you already do in everyday life, it reduces other road users' ability to take you by surprise, and catch you unprepared.

When you meet someone new:

you form an instant impression of them.

This is instinctive and automatic, and includes expectations about how they will behave. Mainly, it is a defence mechanism to weigh up what threat they could be.

It works by recognising the closest fit to "similar" people you have met before.

Imagine standing in a queue between a smartly dressed, prim young woman, and a big brawny chap in rags, with heavy tattoos and a broken nose. Even before the end of the sentence you already had different feelings about these two people.

This is stereotyping, and everyone does it all the time. How "fair" it might be to the individuals is not the question. Most stereotypes exist because:

they reflect true patterns of behaviour.

And they are invaluable for helping us to cope with the uncertainties of life.

Notice too that in storytelling, such as in films or television, the characters are built very quickly in your mind by invoking clear stereotypes. Then sharp twists in the plot are achieved by suddenly contradicting them later.

In driving, just as in any other situation, using stereotypes will help you predict what people might do, and therefore be more prepared for it. This is very powerful because out on the road you "meet" so many people so fleetingly, and:

you need to size them up almost instantly.

Especially vital is to spot who is likely to create risk. Apart from the L-plate, no one wears an overt "flag" of warning. You have to work it out for yourself.

But you already recognise at least some driver types. Consider these two cars, and answer the question:

a new Vauxhall Corsa with 4 grey-haired ladies

an old Ford Escort with 4 lively young lads

What's the difference?

This example usually stirs a wry smile as people realise just how distinctive some drivers are. Already you know something about what to expect from these cars. And that is the key. For many road users, <u>you know what to expect</u>!

Now look at one road user quite closely - cyclists, for example.

<u>Cyclists</u>

- <u>higher viewpoint</u> than most cars
- very manoeuvrable, will <u>weave</u> about in traffic
- <u>misjudge</u> the speed and stopping ability of motor vehicles
    - especially if too young to be a driver
- <u>vary</u> greatly from meandering shopper to determined racer
- <u>distance horizon</u> is short
    - preoccupied with the <u>road surface</u> in front
- <u>will swerve</u> around anything
    - bumps, holes, puddles, drains, traffic calming, etc
- <u>reluctant to brake</u> because of the hard effort lost
- may <u>bend the rules</u> by ignoring red lights, one-way streets, etc
- ride <u>very close</u> in town traffic
- <u>not heard</u> by other road users
- hearing impaired by <u>wind noise</u> in their ears
- <u>no rear view</u>, and vision dramatically impaired by rain
- always trying to <u>balance to two wheels</u>

Even with the number of points shown in the box, there is nothing there that you don't already know about cyclists.

But how much of it do you <u>use</u> when you meet one...?

Similar pictures can be drawn for other groups, that simply collect together what you already know, such as:

Young drivers

- low experience, and unaware of why they have limitations
- much higher crash rates than average
- testosterone in males can turn driving into
  an important jungle contest
- often worst when their mates are on board
- high spirited, with low sensitivity to risk
- thrilled to be mobile
- limited idea of what good driving involves

Pedestrians

- usually excellent visibility and hearing, if they use it
- in a different world, thinking of other things
- they are not part of the traffic
  - they travel across the flow - thus the added danger
- very easily damaged
- look the wrong way in one-way streets
- ignore some rules, such as crossings
- misjudge the speed and stopping ability of traffic
- over 80% are hit in the road, not on a refuge or a crossing
  - 5-15 year old boys are a high risk group
  - as are also male drunks at night
- highly manoeuvrable, to step suddenly into the road

Children

- under 8 years old:
  - immature judgement of distance or speed
  - very easily distracted, and act on impulse
  - more interested in play, little concept of danger
- 9-16 years old:
  - starting to believe they can handle risks
  - vulnerable to peer pressures to take risks
  - still lack experience and easily distracted

Trucks

- have the advantage of a very high viewpoint
- normally quite definite about what they are doing
  - except when lost in an unfamiliar town
- massive weight and momentum
  - taking up to three times as long as a car to stop
- high potential to do damage
- reluctant to brake, because acceleration is so slow
- reluctant to take cruise control off when on major roads
- need a lot of space when turning, so will swing wide
- severe blind spots behind, and below the passenger door

Elderly drivers

- long experience, but probably now low mileage
- more sedentary outlook, no necessity to rush
- find it hard to cope with modern traffic density and speed
- direct effects of aging include:
  - worsening eyesight and hearing
  - less decisive
  - reduced muscle strength
  - stiff joints and restricted movements
  - more likely to be on medications
- higher crash rates than average

White Van Man

- under delivery schedule pressure
- "time is money" style
- likely to force their way through traffic aggressively
- may rely on others to resolve the danger created
- vehicle is often "battle-scarred"
- will accept distractions on the move,
  - such as eating, map-reading and using a phone

Over time you can construct many more than these:
wherever you find repeating patterns in what people do.

Perhaps for men and women, motorcyclists, buses, taxi drivers, school run Mums, left-hand drive vehicles and so on. And within these you may also begin to quickly spot: considerate vs impatient, skilled vs reckless, alert vs inattentive, calm vs nervous, etc.

Indeed, you probably already hold many views about the people you meet on the road. But be careful not to just release a flood of unfounded prejudice - whether your own or someone else's. That would make your anticipation worse, not better.

You should only:
work with your actual experience,
that has been built personally, and then use it privately while you drive.

You may also have heard someone say you should, "Drive as if everyone else is a complete idiot", but this typecasts most people wrongly. To pinpoint the real threats you need to be more selective than that.

Another caution is that, inevitably, you will focus on people's negative points. These are the ones likely to create the most danger. But don't brandish your observations as if to blame people angrily for their incompetence. The purpose is only that:

you become steadily smarter at knowing what others are likely to do.

There is a further big benefit too. Because whatever others around you do, it is much easier to respond <u>calmly</u> if you suspected beforehand that they might do it. That way, even major errors can be coolly taken in your stride.

Fortunately, out on the road:

the people who repeatedly create danger often fit a strong stereotype,

which means that <u>you can learn to spot them</u>!

Finally for you to consider: what do you think other people see when they look at you...?

2.7.2.4 Fast reactions - myth and reality

> **Key point**: **- Fast reactions are less important than
> reacting to the right things.**

Lightning reactions are proof of great skill and a source of worthy pride, right?

This is a popular belief, and we are encouraged to think so.

**But how useful is it to
react quickly?**

And can it reduce the need to anticipate?

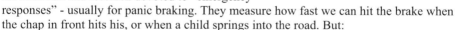

Fast reactions are often said to be an essential driving skill, and the emphasis is reinforced by the attention and research devoted to "emergency responses" - usually for panic braking. They measure how fast we can hit the brake when the chap in front hits his, or when a child springs into the road. But:

for real safety, this comes far down the list of skills.

And the reason is simply that it is far more important, and skilful, to <u>prevent</u> a crisis from occurring, than <u>react</u> to it when it does.

Reacting very quickly is only required to cope with being caught totally unprepared. It may be a reassuring ability to have, but the need to use fast reactions is usually a sign of dramatic failure, not success.

It is dangerous to count fast reactions as a core driving skill.

Unfortunately, many drivers adopt a style that relies on snap decisions and sudden actions. Tailgating is a common example. Perhaps they imagine it displays a heroic talent. But instead it is a truly inept technique that radiates high risk to everyone around.

The effect on the often condemned macho young male is interesting. He is already hormonally charged for a physical challenge, so responds eagerly to the notion that skill is embodied in fast reactions. It gives him a perfect style to flaunt his prowess at the wheel. But in a classic "brawn versus brain" contrast, he has no time to realise that far more control over events is being achieved by drivers with better anticipation.

The vital point is not whether you have "fast" reactions, but:

what are you reacting <u>to</u> ??

Is it the brake lights on the car in front? Or the situation you have seen developing far down the road? How obvious does a threat have to get before you respond?

It is also the difference between reacting to the <u>past</u> (what has already happened), and:

reacting to the <u>future</u> (what is <u>going</u> to happen).

Inevitably, responding to the past requires very fast reactions - and unnecessarily so.

Past events   Future events

So now, "good" and "fast" reactions are totally different things. A response that is early and light is far superior to one that is late and severe. It is much better risk control.

But don't think that reacting gently equates to a sedentary style. It often helps good progress to be made safely. Don't confuse quick thinking with fast reactions either. To rely on fast reactions is more likely to be a sign of slow thinking and a lack of foresight.

Expert drivers will give little thought to the raw speed of their physical reactions. And would certainly not see them as an exalted skill or source of particular pride. What they will prize highly, though, are:

the much more useful powers of anticipation!

2.7.2.5 Surprise horizon

> <u>Key point</u>:   - Using a surprise horizon lets you measure
> your own anticipation.

For many people this is a very simple and powerful idea. It measures how far you can see into the future - and therefore how well you anticipate. It also helps you to judge how threatening a surprise might be.

Your surprise horizon is given by:

**how far away are the events that
you are not predicting?**

It is measured in <u>seconds</u> (approximately!).

A significant surprise is one that changes your actions or intentions. And you simply notice roughly where it is in time away from you.

The event could be a car pulling out five seconds up the road, or a pedestrian stepping into the road just one second away. It could also be something that does not happen, that you were almost certain would. Perhaps someone fails to turn as they were indicating.

Obviously, there are big surprises and small ones, but their closeness is also a very strong factor in the threat they carry. Recall that the major effect of a surprise is to:

rob you of time to plan your actions.

Ideally, the aim would be to predict everything everywhere, but in practice there will often be something you did not foresee. The concept of a surprise horizon puts a laser-sharp focus on surprises that are near to you, rather than distant.

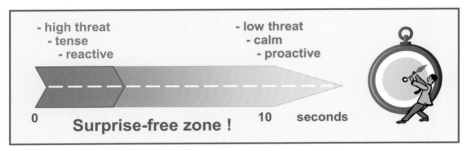

At about 5 seconds, the surprise horizon is good. This usually contains the most vital moments. Maintaining it at:

10 seconds is in expert territory,

with a level of foresight that keeps risk low, and allows calm and smooth progress with proactive control.

Conversely, as your horizon shortens your driving will lose its composure. And the risk will also be compounded by the tension it places you under.

At less than 2-3 seconds, your style will be a stream of rushed reactions

to events and dangers that you are badly prepared for.

Using this technique prompts you to check how sure you are about everything that will happen in the next "about x seconds" of your driving. How far out this can be in practice will vary with the situation, especially if it becomes very busy or something blocks your view. But the vital points are to:

- try to extend your surprise horizon out to about 10 seconds
- be very aware when it is shortened, and you are thrown into pure reacting.

Clearly, adjusting your speed will change your surprise horizon, and this is one of your levers of control. But:

the main control is achieved with your powers of anticipation!

In addition to measuring your anticipation like this on a time scale, other key judgements can be seen as time-based too, such as braking and following-distances, and this is drawn together later under Driving Plans.

2.7.2.6 Being predictable - more revealing

> **Key points:** - **If you surprise someone, they are more likely to hit you.**
>
> - **Don't just signal - be predictable!**

This is a hugely important idea, and starts with a basic question. Who do you think should make sure that other people anticipate what you do?

If you believe it is nearly all their own responsibility, you are missing a big opportunity, and putting yourself in needless danger.

Whenever your actions are unexpected by someone else, it is as dangerous for you as it is for them. Put simply:

> *if you surprise someone, they are more likely to hit you.*

This applies to all road users - even pedestrians. The problem will be that they expected you to do something else, or did not even know you were there.

Let's look further. Why do you signal? This is another vital question.

The Highway Code says:

"to warn and inform other road users of your intended actions".

And this comes with guidance rules for when and how to signal in various circumstances - at junctions or roundabouts, changing lane, and so on.

But is it enough to just give out a signal to "warn and inform"? It can become a quite robotic action, that passes your fate into the hands of someone else.

In many situations, even your signal according to the rules will still leave some of the people around you surprised. Perhaps they could not see the signal, are not very alert, or for some reason just assumed you would do something else. Maybe they were even <u>relying</u> on you to do something else!

However, your safety will be dramatically increased by adopting a much bigger objective than to "warn and inform". It is to simply:

<u>Be predictable!!</u>

These are two tremendously powerful words, once you have grasped their full meaning. They are the reason <u>why</u> so much of what you do is necessary. You just need to <u>be predictable</u> to those around you.

With this objective in your driving, it will inevitably lead to:

- a better understanding of your total situation
- a style that is more involved in what is happening around you
- better searching for the road users who could hit you
- cooperating more to help others anticipate you - and checking that they have
- making all your "signals" consistent (indicators, position, direction, speed, brake lights, horn, where you point your front wheels, where you are looking, etc).

The purpose of being predictable is:

to actively help everyone to adjust safely to what you do.

It highlights again the importance of a positive and purposeful driving style, that leaves no doubt about what is happening. A passive or nervous driver will send mixed signals, and create uncertainty.

Some other important points:

- Because surprise is so dangerous, it is guaranteed to anger other road users probably more than anything else. No matter what errors you make, the element of surprise is instinctively a greater threat. In fact, causing a surprise will often be the error itself.

- You can do unexpected things that otherwise seem to be your "right" to do. For example, going all the way round a small roundabout when you are lost is likely to be a surprise for other traffic.

Or there are things that you fail to do, such as the notorious case of not entering a roundabout when the chap behind thought you would.

Not that you have to resolve this by lunging forward in advance of your judgement. You can simply keep your brake lights on until you decide to actually go.

In other words:

**don't let someone think you are going
to do something you are not.**

- You can also react to an incoming surprise in a way that magnifies it for someone else, such as happens in braking waves along tight-flowing traffic. You should aim to "absorb and reduce" surprises, not increase them.

Fortunately, there are two advantages in the surprises you give out over those that you receive:

- they are under your own control to prevent
- you can change your own driving very quickly.

By contrast, being less surprised by others needs sharp anticipation, which may take a while to gain.

So, although it has such a huge benefit in safety:

being predictable is relatively easy to achieve.

In fact, the first step is instantaneous - you just recognise how important it is. Even this will have an immediate effect on what you think and do. The next step may take a little longer to digest, but is still straightforward. It is for you to:

- consciously help other road users to anticipate you well - early and correctly
- make sure you can resolve any surprises that you do create.

A further bonus is that the fewer surprises you give out, the fewer you will receive too. Surprising someone will often trigger an erratic action back. So being predictable has a gearing effect that ratchets down the level of uncertainty for everyone.

Being seen - look at me!

Naturally, you want all the road users around you to know you are there!

If they don't, they will feel no need to avoid you.

So while expert drivers aim to be unobtrusive in traffic, they still need to be noticed, but they cause less disturbance.

There are simple ways to make sure you don't become invisible:
- Notice when others look at you
  - Especially those who could move directly into your path.
  - Who is not looking at you when they should? Is the driver waiting in a side road looking only the other way? Are the children lingering on the kerb engrossed in another world?
- Don't be afraid to sound your horn to get noticed
  - That is what it is for. And don't leave it too late for anyone to react.
- Use your lights
  - Not only at night, but daytime lights are good practice too - especially if visibility is reduced or your car is a dull colour, or when the sun casts dark shadows under trees.
- If necessary, adjust your road position to deliberately show yourself
  - A specific purpose of your road position is to ensure you can be seen (see The Purpose of Position in the section on Space later).
  - As you move forward into new situations, be aware that some people may not have seen you coming.
- Recognise other vehicle's blind spots
  - Know when you are moving into one, and try not to stay there.
  - Notice them especially where traffic is changing lanes at merge-points, or flows are crossing at roundabouts or junctions.
  - Notice left-hand drive vehicles, and that their blind spots are reversed.
  - Be aware of the spectacular side-swipes that big trucks inflict on cars that sit in the blind spot below their passenger door.
- Be aware of pedestrians' blind spots too
  - You can easily be hidden from their view, such as behind a parked lorry.
  - Or people might be reluctant to look directly into heavy rain.

Being understood - every move you make

After being seen, you need to be correctly understood too. You definitely can't assume that someone knows what you intend to do:

just because they can see you.

Most drivers will cooperate with you, providing they know clearly what you want to do, and if they can easily adjust to it. Certainly, some people cooperate badly, but you will make it harder by being vague.

Whether we mean to or not, we all "radiate" intentions all of the time. Your speed, position and direction, for example, all contain implied information about what you will do next.

Some people will read all of the clues very well, but others will notice only the formal signals that are used.

Giving off the wrong, or confusing, signals will create surprise.

Vitally, you should always be thinking about who needs information from you and why. Sometimes it may simply be a courtesy to remove any doubts they may have. But:

all of your signals should have a specific aim.

Your communication will vary as you drive, using a combination of:

- **Direction indicators** - should be early enough to show the intention, not just confirm what is already being done. They are not required if you are certain that no one is there to benefit - but only if totally <u>certain</u>.
- **Hazard indicators** - if you are temporarily causing an obstruction, or use them also on fast roads to warn those behind of danger ahead.
- **Brake lights** - are the most frequent light signal you give, but rarely used as a conscious one. Use it <u>before</u> braking to warn someone that is following too closely, or to tell someone behind that you are staying stationary.
- **Hand signals** - rarely used these days, except those that do not involve opening the window, which usually takes too long. The most useful is probably the open-palm courtesy sign to show thanks for some help, or to apologise for an error.
- **Horn** - to give an audible warning where you cannot be seen, such as round a narrow blind bend, or to someone not paying attention.
- **Headlight flashes** - often used, but risk being misunderstood. To be used with great care, if at all. The meaning depends on the precise situation, and ranges from a courteous, "After you...", to the impatient, "Get out of the way!!". So it is easy to increase uncertainty rather than reduce it. The approved use in the Highway Code is only to alert others to your presence.
- **Position, direction and speed** - this is your continuous "road language", and is often overlooked as a vital communication. It radiates a definite "look" to what you are doing. And:

even small changes will have a
strong meaning to those who are alert.

- **Front wheels** - give a strong signal, especially when you are stationary and about to move off. Point them where you want to go. The exception is to leave them straight if you are waiting to turn across oncoming traffic and could get shunted forward from behind.
- **Where you look** - will be noticed by observant people, even from behind, so try not to be misleading at a critical moment. Making eye contact with someone also tells them they have been noticed. In most situations, it will confuse people if you are not looking where you want to go, or at an obvious source of danger. Staring in a shop window at a busy junction, for example, does not help.

Above all, know that:

as you observe others, they are also observing you,

and trying to work out what you will do. So it helps to identify who you are in danger from if they do <u>not</u> know what you are going to do. And try to have a simple and consistent style, that is easy for others to understand, and just **be predictable!**

2.7.2.7 Driving plans - thinking ahead

> **Key points:** - **Planning ahead is the only way to control events, and what happens to you.**
>
> - **Failing to plan increases your uncertainties and risks.**

The third type of surprise is the self-inflicted kind, and this gets denied most strongly.

Quite rightly, people see it as not a sensible thing to do. But they do it anyway while being unaware, and blame others for the effects. Let's explore.

How could you create surprise for yourself? It happens very easily by:

- not paying attention
- having only vague intentions
- taking actions with an uncertain outcome.

The effect is to:

increase the unexpected in an almost "negative anticipation".

You also become less predictable to others, since you cannot communicate your intentions without first knowing them definitely yourself. So you radiate more surprises outwards too. Inevitably all of this makes you more vulnerable.

Thinking ahead

It is common to see driving mistakes in terms of doing something wrong with the physical controls - the steering or pedals. But there is a much bigger error when:

> control over events is abandoned by not thinking ahead.

The ability to plan well ahead is a major difference between good and bad drivers. As we saw before, poor skill is often centred on reacting to what <u>has</u> already happened - the past. Whereas, planning ahead increases your control of what <u>will</u> happen - the future. Even in congested traffic you should not be forced into sudden action.

How to stop creating surprise for yourself is easy to explain, but takes a while to achieve. It begins when you start to think about <u>your own part</u> in what will happen next.

This is called your "driving plan". But there is no mystique in that term. It is simply:

> knowing what you intend to do for the
> next few moments of driving.

And these intentions roll forward naturally as you make progress. Behind the driving plan is one of your main decision processes, as you decide how you are going to get safely through the next 10-15 seconds of driving. In doing this:

> successful planning relies on
> excellent observation and good risk assessment,

as the Driving Process showed before. The observation must give you information as early as possible, which definitely involves "raising your vision" beyond the vehicle in front and scanning into the distance. It also includes anticipating what other road users might do, and detecting hazards that you cannot directly see.

And all of this must then be assessed for the risks that you need to deal with, and their influence on what you intend to do. Certainly:

> there is little point is detecting a hazard without
> deciding what to do about it.

The classic approach to driving plans uses three questions to lead your thinking through stages about the possible threats:

- what can be seen?
- what cannot be seen?
- what may reasonably be expected to happen?

They apply all the time - whether you want to overtake, need to cross a busy roundabout, are caught up in thick traffic, or are just driving along a quiet road.

For instance, what would you plan to do in the following situation, taken from real life? It happens to be quite a short timescale example - all over in a few seconds.

You are the blue car in the next scene on a two-lane dual carriageway, doing 60mph behind a lorry. A battle-scarred decorator's van overtakes you, with a large ladder on the roof-rack. As it turns in front of the lorry <u>you see</u> the ladder begin to swing out at the back. Then the van <u>disappears</u> from view. So what <u>may happen</u> next?

What will you do - calmly and under control?

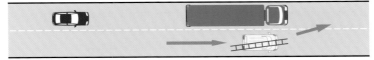

Do you wait to see what happens? Will the lorry driver panic? Will a mangled ladder appear on the road? Should you brake immediately - and how hard? Do you know what is behind - in both lanes? How close are you travelling anyway?

Even more importantly, did you spot the ladder as a hazard as the van went past, and start thinking ahead five seconds ago? Or did you lose that time?

Recall the causes of danger: Speed, Surprise and Space. They all play vital roles as this situation unfolds.

As it happened, this driver handled the situation well. He dropped right back, and moved out to go around the debris when it came through a few seconds later. He already knew (all round awareness) there was space behind, and could act quickly in safety. His instincts were also put on alert by the state of the van as it went past.

The time dimension

The most important thing for safety is to have time to think and act. And the essence of good planning is:

to create enough time, and use it well.

How far you can usefully plan forward will depend on the situation. But something interesting happens when we see a "time dimension" running through each of the three factors of risk:

- Speed — stopping ability (see Maximum Braking)
- Surprise — surprise horizon (see Surprise Horizon)
- Space — following distance (see The Golden Rule).

Putting them together on the same axis makes a striking picture, combining the key elements of braking, anticipation and position. It shows how crucial time is in managing risk, and confirms again that all the sources of risk must be balanced together.

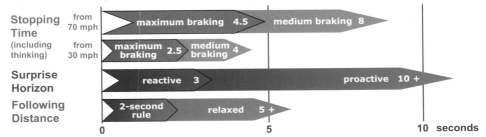

We also see graphically why most trainers advise a span of about 10 seconds for a good driving plan. Beyond 10 seconds your intentions will inevitably be more changeable, especially in thick or fast traffic where it matters most.

A good plan

So what makes a <u>good</u> driving plan? Remember that the purpose is to help you think ahead and cover the risks. And in a manner that is proactive, smooth and relaxed.

Here are some pointers for a good plan:

	Good	Poor
Time span	Covers the next 10 seconds or so. This usually contains the critical moments of action, plus time to think ahead and be well prepared.	Too short: "I am just keeping a 2-second gap from the car in front". This is also fixated on a single object. Too long: "I am going straight over the next two roundabouts, then left at the junction about a mile ahead to join the motorway southbound". This is about navigating, not driving.
Risks	Identifies the risks: "I need to slow, and watch the fast stream of traffic flowing into the roundabout from the left. But there is nothing coming from straight ahead or the right".	Ignores the risks: "The roundabout is busy, and I am going straight across".
Decisions	Is about <u>what</u> you intend to do, and the decisions involved: "I am holding back to space off the car in front that is slowing to turn left. I will then move forward again and check if it is still clear to pass the next one up, bearing in mind there is a bend in the far distance". The main focus is rightly outside the car, and your thinking is about what you want the car to do.	Concentrates on <u>how</u> to make the car do what you want, by operating the controls: "I have checked my rear mirror and am braking gently. I will then change down to second gear to accelerate again, and stay in that gear and steer towards the centre of the road, hoping to overtake". Using the controls should be quite automatic, so that what you do inside the car does not need a lot of thought.
Responsive	Responds to changing events, and the constant input from your observation and risk assessment.	Sticks stubbornly to a course of action that has been decided.
Achievable	Is simple, and within your control.	Relies on things outside your control going right. Requires sudden action if they do not.
Options	Includes more than one option for events to unfold in different ways. This is the "what if" part of your planning: "I am increasing speed, but if the car behind pulls out to pass, I will hold back to make it easier for him to go through".	Has only a single course of action: "I am accelerating down the clear road".

Never imagine, though, that your plans should be forced into coherent mental sentences. Time is much too short for such a huge "verbal" distraction to your natural flow of thinking.

Remember that experts use intuition, that works very fast and without language, and it is enough to:

simply "know" your intentions at the intuitive level.

Summary

Forward thinking and a good driving plan gives you more control over risk and what happens to you by:

- creating more time to decide what to do
- improving anticipation and concentration
- identifying early any conflicts with what others might do
- avoiding the stress and danger of rushed decisions.

Expert drivers are so relaxed largely because they:

do very little that has not already been calmly planned before.

The driving plan is where your intuitive "feel" for danger moves forward into decision-making. Thinking ahead helps you to naturally balance the causes of risk.

The main thing is to have:

a rolling set of active decisions about what you intend to do.

2.7.3 Space

> **Key points:** - Increasing space dramatically lowers risk.
>
> - Road space is to be shared, not hogged as a piece of "personal territory".
>
> - Good use of space is a sign of many other skills too.

Space is easy to see, but most drivers use it badly - either clumsily or selfishly. And it is not simply because some people have naturally better spatial awareness.

It shows in poor positioning, traffic crushed tighter than it needs to be, or drivers stubbornly hogging space that someone else needs. Indeed, many crashes that are blamed on speed would be better seen as poor use of space. Remember that crashes happen because someone runs out of room, and better use of space can dramatically cut risk.

Recalling the model again:

$$\text{Risk} \quad = \quad \frac{\text{Speed} \quad x \quad \text{Surprise}}{\boxed{\text{Space}}}$$

As we know, more space means less risk - so space is good. It is very good! And the constant question here is:

"How much room do I have available to use, and share?"

This is about your need for space, and everyone else's around you too. All of the needs must coexist.

However, you may rarely give this much specific thought. Apart from the distance to the vehicle in front, motorists are taught little about space. But the way that a driver uses road-space can be a revealing sign of overall skill. Good use of space is closely connected to also having good observation, anticipation and control.

Standing back for a moment, the space around us has a deeply personal significance that is about freedom of movement. Life itself is fundamentally about being free and able to move around.

In nature, animals fight fiercely over territories to protect food sources and breeding grounds.

So in over-crowded conditions, normally friendly contact instinctively becomes more aggressive.

In a similar way, even as "civilised humans" we are:

not well equipped for living in large dense communities.

Especially important is the forced proximity to strangers. We all have "personal space" that we want to protect, and the closer people get the more intrusive it is.

Restricting someone's movement or space is therefore openly threatening, and will shift their behaviour towards being more agitated, and perhaps even violent. Notice too, that denying people space is used as a form of punishment in the justice system.

It is not surprising, therefore, that space has been called the "ultimate luxury", and the enjoyment of many holidays is in simply regaining the freedom of wide open spaces.

This gives us:

a new perspective on some common road behaviour.

Perhaps it is easier now to see why practices like lane-hogging, cutting-in and tailgating arouse such immense anger. They are always high on the list in surveys of drivers' pet hates. Congestion too, has a clearly more profound effect on people than just delaying journeys. Especially when it is caused by poor use of space rather than just traffic volume.

So then, our feelings about space are easier to understand by recognising three things:

- the importance of freedom of movement
- the car as a piece of "mobile territory"
- the need for personal space.

In addition, there is the knowledge that, by definition:

having <u>enough</u> space will protect you from all collisions,

and in this sense, space is the most precious commodity on the road.

It may sound strange, but we can also learn a lot from artists. Usually, people look at a scene and see only the objects. But to an artist, the spaces are just as vital - because they define where the objects are in relation to each other.

For drivers, space has equal importance because it separates the objects from impact as they move around.

What we learn, therefore, is to study the spaces carefully too, for the part they are playing.

Clearly, deciding what is "enough" space is the challenge, together with how to create it. And also, how spaces are <u>changing</u> can be more important than simply how big they are.

All of this means that:

developing a sharp instinct for space is a vital part of your risk sense.

2.7.3.1 Types of space

> <u>Key point</u>:   - Understanding "threatened" space is
>   crucial to assessing risk.

In everyday life, we see space in a very simple way - it is either empty or full. But for road users most of the problem is caused because:

> movable objects cast danger into the spaces around them.

And that changes everything. We saw before, when discussing speed (see The Golden Rule), that a space being "empty" does not necessarily mean it is "clear" and safe to use.

This is resolved by the idea of "threatened" space - with a gradient of risk between the space being free and occupied:

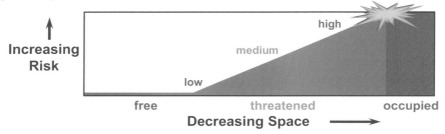

Occupied space is the easiest to see and understand. It is where the objects are, and we can't go there. The purpose then is to gauge the degree of threat that is present in the other spaces. Un-occupied space can be assessed to be either "free" or "threatened".

Free space

Although it may be increasingly hard to find in modern traffic, we can define space as "free" if:

> entering it carries a negligible risk of collision.

Within this we can see further types of free space, for example:

- **"Wasted" space**

  This happens when traffic crushes itself together instead of using space that is easily available. The blue car in this scene is just cruising, with no intention of overtaking even though there may be opportunities.

Dropping back into the space behind would dramatically lower the risk for all three of the bunched group. Similarly, the silver car could try moving forward to test whether the others really are fixated on bumpers.

- **"Shielded" space**

  Vehicles are often protected by other traffic. Here, the blue car can emerge, shielded by the slow turning lorry.

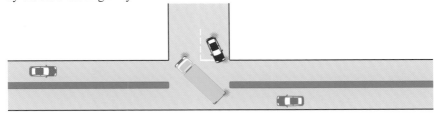

  Similar effects occur in many junction situations, and if anticipated correctly can be used to safe advantage. But always be aware of the speed of the traffic that could come through after the protection moves away.

- **"Escape route" space**

  In an emergency, you may need to steer abruptly to avoid a collision (see also Escape Routes later). Potential escape routes will lie to each side of your current direction. Note that normally prohibited space <u>can</u> be used in emergencies - such as hatched areas.

Threatened space

Any space you want to enter is threatened if:

someone else could get there too.

They may be moving or stationary, but you must judge and prepare for the likelihood that they could be there at the same time as you.

> In this scene, if you were the blue car, are you entering "free" space, because it is empty and everyone else should wait for you to go through?

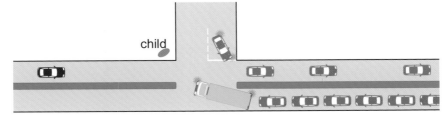

Definitely not. It has several threats that you should have already prepared for.

At a minimum you should have checked behind, be covering the brake, ensuring everyone has seen you, and checking for any movement in the pedestrian's legs or the vehicle's wheels. And possibly started to brake too, depending on your speed.

Notice the part played by good observation, and how the threat to space naturally prompts more attention to speed and surprise (anticipation).

The most obvious high risk is in the area that a vehicle cannot avoid entering by virtue of its speed and direction. This is at least its shortest stopping distance, and more if the driver is not alert.

We could call this the "committed" space. And we know that anything here is certain to be hit - unless it is moving away. So in situations such as a tailgating convoy, impacts are only avoided if everyone continues the steady motion. If someone touches the brake, the risk shoots up.

Although committed space is quite easy to identify, the biggest problem is that:

too many people choose to ignore the threat!

It is also interesting to observe how people treat space they cannot see into, such as blind bends or over the brow of a hill. It seems rational to assume some degree of threat, but more often than not people drive on with an apparent certainty that it is free.

Threats can change very rapidly, of course, and as traffic moves around:

a strong signal is given by whether spaces are "opening" or "closing".

A space is higher risk if it is closing than if it is opening, and this is a vital thing for drivers to notice.

Studying other people's space also gives your anticipation an extra edge too. For example, if the car in front of you is close to the one in front of it, is it more likely to brake suddenly?

Or, have you ever seen a driver on the inside lane of a motorway suddenly realise they are closing fast on a slow lorry - and lunge out before looking? Seeing the closing space would have told you this was likely to happen. You will find that many drivers get themselves dangerously "boxed in" like this.

Conversely, drivers can be slow to recognise the opportunity when space is opening up. This may be, for example, someone who is keen to pass the vehicle in front, but fails to anticipate and prepare for when the road becomes clear.

All of this, taken together, means that by understanding threatened space:

you will build much stronger defences.

And this will include defences against other road users who get into danger, and are likely to act suddenly.

2.7.3.2 The purpose of position

> **Key points**:   - You manage space by choosing your road position.
>
>   - Give space to danger - that is what it is for!

Safe and efficient travel on the road is largely about smooth traffic flow. And this, in turn, depends on drivers fitting themselves well into the traffic. Dangerous disruptions in flow can usually be traced back to a vehicle with poor position. But:

few drivers think about placing their car precisely.

Most seem content to wander quite randomly within the space they "claim" to be theirs. Or they hypnotically line up neatly behind whatever is in front.

Some rules from basic training might also still be exerting an influence, such as:

- "Keep one metre from the kerb", as some students are told
- on a left-hand bend, "Keep to the centre of your lane as you approach. Don't move to the centre of the road to improve your view"
- on motorways, "Keep your vehicle steady in the centre of the lane".

At advanced level, the advice is more flexible, and it is better to think that:

your road position has a definite purpose.

The first step, though, is to add a second dimension to the commonly understood definition of position:

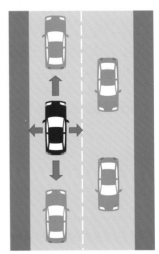

1. **Side-to-side**

   This is the usual meaning of position. It is your distance from the kerb and centre of the road, or from the edges of your lane.

   We control it mainly by steering, although using the accelerator or brakes in a bend can also alter the line you take.

2. **Front-to-back**

   This is the other component of your position in the traffic.

   Accelerating or braking (including engine braking) controls your distance to the vehicles in front and behind.

Taken together, these two dimensions are your full road position.

Now let's look at what this position should be achieving for you. Inevitably, it will be a compromise between conflicting needs. But a number of things come together here, and:

**you should never underestimate
the value of controlling your position.**

The purpose of where you place yourself in the traffic should include:

- **A safe way forward**

  This is the clearest overall purpose, and the top priority. Your position must allow you to proceed without collision!

- **See and be seen**

  You need a commanding view of your driving scene, and to ensure that others can see you too.

  Your view can be obscured, for example, by being too close to the vehicle in front. And your line of sight round bends is improved by entering left-hand bends close to the crown, and close to the verge for right-hand bends.

  And, yet again, don't <u>stay</u> in the blind spots of other vehicles, of course.

- **Give space to danger**

  More than anything else, this is what space is for! Giving a bit more room to threats and uncertainties is a powerful way to build a safety margin around you. Sometimes this is called creating a "cushion" or "buffer" around yourself to absorb mistakes.

  If there are hazards on both sides, such as parked cars and oncoming traffic, take a middle course between them, balanced on the risks.

  Also, use the simple "hold-back" technique to adjust your arrival into situations that need more time to resolve themselves, such as traffic that is slow to clear a junction.

- **Following distance**

  This is a strong case of giving space to danger. Treat the area in front as your "life-space". To be gruesomely blunt, if you die on the road, it is likely to be here. A third of all crashes are rear shunts - so be sure not to create one!.

  Backing off a little further will often also compensate for poor use of space elsewhere, such as the traffic ahead being tightly bunched, or the chap behind riding on your bumper. The extra space in front will regain your control of the risks.

  Conversely, the habit of drivers who leave a sub-second gap at high speed is like loading a gun and fiddling idly with the trigger.

- **Signal intentions**

  Make sure that your position confirms your intentions, and adds to your being predictable. To signal right and position to the left, for example, is confusing. Or if you tailgate, it can look like the intention to pass.

- **Reducing bends**

  You can improve control in bends by slightly straightening the line you take to reduce the sideways forces. But keep within your safe road space.

- **Preparing to pass**

  Moving up to pass must sacrifice the following distance, but only temporarily, and with very high attention. Assessing the opportunity to pass should be done from further back.

- **Escape routes**

  In many situations you should create options to swerve safely if it became necessary (see Escape Routes in the next section). Your position must allow you to reach the escape route without hitting something on the way, such as clipping the back corner of the car in front.

- **Vision for others**

  Help others to "see and be seen" too. If possible, try to let the car behind see the traffic in front of you. Anything that improves their anticipation is safer for you.

- **Give space to others**

  Do not deny someone else the space they need - either unreasonably or maliciously. Road space is there to be shared, and contests over it will only create anger and invite collisions. Especially, you should allow some room for others to make errors.

  You can also cooperate powerfully by anticipating when someone else needs more space, such as moving over to let someone enter a motorway, or seeing that a turning lorry needs to swing wide.

A few examples will illustrate some of these points:

- The tightness of the queue behind the lorry here serves no purpose at all. The blue car, especially has no chance of passing, and has space to simply drop back.

- In this motorway scene, the outside lane is far too full and compressed - as is common. If you are the blue car, the ones in front of you are neatly lined up in the centre of the lane.

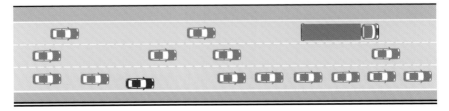

  Because they can't see the brake lights up the line, they can react only to the one directly in front. You, however, have positioned slightly to the outside, which makes a huge difference.

You can now see up the line, and react earlier and smoothly to any braking ahead. Those further back can now see your brake lights too. Possibly, you have also allowed the red driver to see past you on the inside. Even more, in an emergency, you now have better access to an escape route down the wide outer shoulder in this case, which would leave more room for the cars behind to use.

The red car could also gain further by offsetting their position the other way, towards the inside of the lane. All of these benefits come from you, in the blue car, just moving slightly to one side. Offset traffic is safer than neatly aligned.

- Next we have two drivers, each preparing to pass a parked car.

First, the red car's approach is close to the kerb. So when it reaches the parked car it must turn sharply, and point threateningly at the green one, who brakes and swerves in surprise. The red driver also has all the steering work to do when space is tightest.

Conversely, the blue car has already positioned out to the centre line. This signals its intentions early and clearly. The oncoming traffic has already adjusted to let it through and still flow smoothly, and its steering is straight and stable as it passes the obstacle. The driver can also see beyond the parked car for any other hazards. If the oncoming cars did not move over, it has time to simply hold back until they pass.

In all of this, though, there are two important cautions:

1. Be aware that the <u>change</u> in your position sends out a message, as well as the position itself. So try to alter your position subtly, and avoid giving a false signal.

2. Avoid taking positions that are too extreme, and might be hard to recover from quickly if something goes wrong. They might also annoy anyone who doesn't understand your reasons.

Also, since so many drivers do it so badly, be prepared to find that:

skilful use of space may be a lonely endeavour.

And frustrating too if someone takes advantage and destroys the low risk you are trying to maintain. But against that, recall that continually building safety out of other people's danger is what the expert driver does best!

Expert drivers are always thinking about their position, and:

place themselves deliberately, based on the balance of risk.

Indeed, this is <u>how</u> they actively control the space component of risk. They also find that close attention to road position often allows them to make better progress too.

2.7.3.3 Escape routes

> <u>Key points</u>: - **Look for an escape route if you are entering a highly threatened space.**
>
> - **If there isn't one, it should change your risk assessment.**

You should be a bit reluctant to read this section, because it is a "failure strategy". All your best skills have failed, and an impact is suddenly looming that braking alone will not avoid. Emergency steering is your only hope.

The purpose of an escape route is to:
> **add steering to your options in a crisis.**

It is an extreme case of using your road position to control risk - a last resort. By the definition of a crisis, at this stage all your options are likely to be high risk.

Perhaps a van springs out of a junction in front of you, or a cyclist swerves violently around a pothole you hadn't seen in the fading light. Suddenly you must find more space.

Some people take evasive action instinctively when necessary, but others freeze and "lock-on" to the target they want to avoid. Sometimes action is taken that makes matters worse. No matter how much you want to be someone who would handle emergencies coolly, you will only find out when actually tested. But your chances will certainly be better for thinking it through beforehand.

The need to locate an escape route arises:
> **whenever you are entering a highly threatened space.**

"What would I do if that pedestrian stepped off the kerb?", and so on. Inevitably, though, you will find that an escape route often does not exist at all - perhaps even in most situations. And this is a crucial part of your overall assessment of risk.

Let's look at some examples:

- In this scene, the jostling children are an <u>indirect</u> threat. If one of them is pushed into the road, the red car will swerve away.

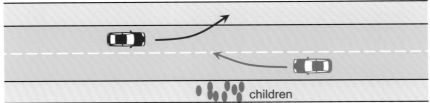

children

The blue car must then go left to avoid a head-on impact, possibly mounting the footpath - if it is clear, and the kerbstones are not too high.

- At this junction, the green car comes out of the side road, having totally misjudged the blue car, who must take evasive action.

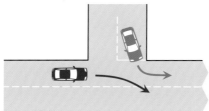 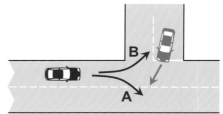

In the first case, the green car turns left, suddenly, and without leaving enough time.

The blue car will probably have to swerve right to miss it - assuming the road is clear of oncoming traffic.

In the second case, the green car is turning right instead, and blue has to choose between two options. With no oncoming traffic, he can again swerve right (A) - but this relies on green braking again to a halt.

If he goes left (B) it assumes green will come out far enough to leave a viable space behind.

To make these decisions quickly, blue must have already weighed up the options as he assessed the junction. If you see other scenarios, it has worked in getting you thinking about the possibilities. Clearly, the green car can still choose a moment to emerge that forces a collision anyway.

- On this fast bend, heavy braking ahead catches the blue driver by surprise - a deer has leapt out up ahead.

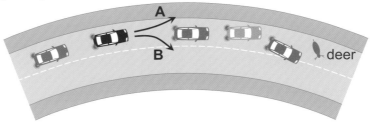

Swerving left on to the verge (A) is easier to do since it turns out of the bend - which is the way the car naturally wants to go. Trying to swerve right (B) is more difficult, because it tightens into the bend. So the bend and the forces already on the car will affect how easily the options can be used.

Important points about escape routes:

- **Extreme action**

  Using an escape route is an emergency reaction to avoid an impending impact. It is in total contrast to the routine steering action that is your proactive adjustment in road position to keep risk low.

- **Safer space**

  The identified space must be a safer option than the impact being avoided. To miss hitting the car in front but create a head-on crash, or to plough into a group of pedestrians, is not a good exchange of dangers. Remember that areas of road that are normally prohibited <u>can</u> be used in an emergency.

- **Accessible space**

  You must be able to get to your escape route. Clipping the corner of another vehicle on the way will probably just spin you across the road - especially if it is bigger than yours. Often only minor changes in position will make an escape route accessible or not. Some escape routes may only be available, and needed, for very brief moments.

- **Under control**

  Any emergency action should still be under good control. To wrench the wheel violently and trust to luck is to be reckless at the worst possible time. For rapid and robust steering, that is still accurate and controlled, the key is in the preparation.

  Mentally, this means thinking through and planning the "what ifs". And physically it is largely about having an effective grip on the wheel. A crisis offers no time to start assessing the situation or to find a proper hold for vigorous action.

  Without doubt, lack of preparation allows many avoidable crashes to happen. Being well prepared should enable you to start steering at the same time as, or even before, you can hit the brake.

- **Look at safety**

  It is well-known that our instincts in a crisis are to steer where we are looking - "the hands follow the eyes". So you must look where you <u>want</u> to go, and <u>not</u> at what you want to avoid. It can be difficult to unglue your eyes from a solid threat, but locking your stare onto the danger is likely to freeze the wheel in the same direction.

- **Practice**

  How to prepare effectively for emergencies is always a problem. And harder here than with braking. You will never get the chance to rehearse realistic evasive action on the road - it is far too risky to do in public.

  So again, training courses off the public roads are highly recommended. Look for one that does "lane-change" manoeuvres, which is a classic, well-controlled evasion (and good fun!). This will only be a short burst of experience, but you will still get a good feel for what is possible - and impossible. And you will certainly be convinced of why you need a good steering grip!

  On the road, you can only use "mental rehearsal". This means looking away into an imagined escape route and visualising yourself steering into it. But do this only when there is no real threat, and the opportunity is safe, otherwise the rehearsal will become an actual performance!

Although the primary aim of your skills is to keep risk low enough to not need escape routes, you can't avoid entering highly threatened spaces sometimes. So don't forget that:

the absence of a viable escape route should alter your assessment of risk.

2.7.4 Consequences

> **Key point:** - The severity of a potential impact shows you the safety margin needed in preventing it.

As you control the elements of risk, the severity of potential crashes should determine the safety margins you try to achieve.

Recall that in the Sense of Danger chapter we used an example. If you suddenly meet a tight bend on a wet night there is a certain chance that you might skid off the road. But if the edge is a flat grass verge the scenario is different to it being a sheer mountain drop. Your problem is rather different in each case:

and your thoughts will be very different too!

So when managing the probability of collision, the more severe a crash would be, the more certain you want to be that it will not happen. And this leads to the extended risk model, by adding Consequences into the balance:

$$\text{Risk} \; = \; \frac{\text{Speed} \; \times \; \text{Surprise}}{\text{Space}} \; \times \; \boxed{\text{Consequences}}$$

The consequences are the degree of damage to people and property:

with people counting much higher than property, of course!

And there are typically two things that determine the level of damage, that are variable at the scene:

- what is hit — the objects involved
- how hard — which is governed by the impact speed.

In an easily memorable form, this is:

$$\text{Consequences} \; = \; \text{Objects} \; \times \; \text{Impact Speed}$$

The following pages examine these two elements as:

- Objects of collision
- Speed of impact.

2.7.4.1 Objects of collision

> **Key point:**   - Out on the road there are many things you could hit, each with very different consequences.

The importance of <u>what</u> would be hit in a crash is obvious. Your own vehicle would be one thing, but it might collide with a car, a truck, a tree, a brick wall, or a child, and so on. All have different consequences.

This is a grisly topic that you will perhaps be less willing to think about, but many crashes that happen are unnecessarily severe.

The question here is:

what objects would be involved
in the crash,
and how easily are they damaged?

This means thinking about both sides of the impact: what you would hit, and also yourself.

In some cases there will be trade-offs between them:

- **Consequences for others**
    - Injury to people is the highest level of consequence. The overriding priority is to protect people, even if it means more damage to property.
    - Especially vulnerable are those who are not inside a vehicle - pedestrians, cyclists and motorcyclists. They account for nearly half of all deaths and serious injuries.
    - If you can't avoid hitting another car, be aware that the doors are a soft spot, and could easily let you through into the passenger space.
    - If you drive a large vehicle, know that your potential to do damage is greater.

- **Consequences for you** - and your car and passengers
    - Again, the priority is to protect people, and for example, if you are shunted from behind it will usually be better to hold the brakes on hard to limit forces on the occupants, even though it may do more damage to your car.
    - Be aware of the huge differences between hitting something coming towards you, against something going in the same direction. This is important too in the next section on Speed of Impact.

- Especially lethal is hitting objects that do not give at all, such as walls and trees. Next in line are big vehicles that don't move when hit by a car, but will hopefully deform a little. A parked car, though stationary, will move and deform when hit. At the bottom of the scale are easily movable things such as small hedges and fences.

- Remember that your car is probably strongest at the front, and weakest at the sides. Crumple zones at the front and rear are designed to absorb impacts, but the doors have far less strength.

- Remember too that any load you have on board should be well secured, and not to have other loose objects that could turn into missiles.

- A glancing blow that allows you to keep going for some distance is usually better than hitting something that stops you dead in your tracks.

- Although choosing your car is not an actual driving decision, it is an important choice. The bigger ones usually offer more protection - but also inflict more harm on others. Some aspects of design play a major role too, and the NCAP crashworthiness ratings can be useful when considering what to buy.

Clearly, crashes vary enormously, from bodywork scratches to fatal injuries. And no one knows how much real control, if any, you might have over a collision after it became inevitable. It would depend on what options you had, how coolly you could act in the circumstances, and most of all how well your thinking had prepared you for the decisions.

What is clear, though, is that:

a slight change in the crash could make

a huge difference to the outcome.

And this might even be a life or death difference, which makes it worth some thought.

It is difficult to regard anything here as a "skill" to be acquired, since no one is expert at having crashes. However, the thinking is similar to identifying escape routes that we saw earlier. But this time there is no totally safe space available.

So although you get some warning as the risk begins to rise, there is a split second when:

the aim suddenly switches

from "crash avoidance" to "damage limitation".

2.7.4.2 Speed of impact

> **Key point:**   - **The likely damage in a crash rises rapidly with the speed of impact.**

Although man has dramatically broken free of his biological limit on speed, the body remains just as fragile - and the machines can be pretty weak too.

Once the impacting objects have "selected" themselves, the damage suffered in a crash hinges on the forces generated (other than factors such as fire, that are at the whim of the gods). And most of this is determined by how fast the objects come together.

The vital question is:

what forces will be exerted on the vehicles and people involved?

The important thing is the <u>rate of change</u> of speed during the impact.

This is what creates the forces that absorb the energy in the motion.

And what matters, therefore, is not the absolute speed, but the <u>relative</u> speed of the objects at impact.

If you hit a stationary object, such as a wall, the relative speed and absolute speed are the same. But when both objects are moving, the relative speed is a combination of the two motions. If two cars meet head-on, one doing 55mph and the other 60mph, the impact is a 115mph explosion of bits! And the effect on each will depend on their comparative weights. Conversely, if they are going in the same direction, the actual impact speed is a 5mph nudge with little damage.

Also, as we saw before (see Seven Deceptions of Speed in the Speed section earlier), the damage potential of speed is deceptive, and rises disproportionately with impact speed. So a 60mph impact is likely to cause far more than twice the damage of a 30mph one.

For example, pedestrian survival rates for different impacts have been published as:
- 95% at 20mph
- 80% at 30mph
- 10% at 40mph

This is similar to the deception on braking distances. Which makes sense, because the impact is acting as a "brake".

The gruesome mechanism of motor collisions is that they unfold in three stages of damage and injury:

1. Vehicle-to-object impacts

This is the first thing that happens, and can be lessened by crumple zones, and "pedestrian-friendly" design.

2. Vehicle-to-occupant impacts

These create cuts and fractures, and can be lessened by seatbelts, airbags, safety cells and cabin interior design. Also at this stage are "momentum" injuries, such as the common "whiplash" of the neck as it strains to hold back the heavy head.

3. Body internal impacts

These occur when bone structures and body organs clash together in very hard impacts. At the scene of a crash, many of these injuries might not be apparent to the untrained eye.

As a little background, although interest in car safety only really took off after the 1950's, many of the devices, such as crumple zones and seatbelts, date back much further to crash testing done to protect pilots after the experiences in World War I.

However, all the safety measures that lessen impact injuries have always worked in exactly the same way. They <u>reduce the forces</u> on the people by lengthening the time of the changes in speed. Whether it is a crumple zone that deforms by a couple of feet, or the fraction of an inch gained by a soft steering wheel, the aim is the same. The central problem to overcome is that the human body reacts badly to the extreme g-forces that are involved in very rapid changes in speed.

In closing this chapter, though, and on a much more positive note, never forget that your highest priorities in driving must be:

the skills that will <u>prevent</u> the collision happening at all!

Skill 8: Car control

Key points: - **Your car must always do what you want it to do. This is "full and reliable" control.**

- **You should know your car's capability. There is little point in a car being able to avoid a crash if the driver cannot make it do so.**

Having good physical control of your car is not only essential, it is a condition of being allowed to use public roads. It is an obvious requirement for safety, and is non-negotiable.

"Good control" means being able to:

make the car do exactly what you want it to.

If your car fails to do what you decided it should, then you have lost some degree of control. How good your decisions are about what to do is a matter for the other chapters! In this skill, we are only concerned with the execution of your decisions.

So this is the physical action part of driving, which is the "end of the line" in the process.

Mainly, it is about operating the controls that determine where the car goes, and when, and how fast.

That is, the major controls: steering, accelerator, brake and gears/clutch.

Recall that this is going to be a brief chapter, because it is one of the three skills that are already a major and essential part of traditional driver training. (The other two are Rules and Regulations, and Fitness Check).

But there are still important points to make, because it is very common for drivers to:

adopt a style that loses vital seconds in their ability to take action.

This applies especially when emergency action is needed, and is in quite simple points about how the brakes and steering are used. And certainly, when we take such care to gain precious fractions of a second with our alertness and observation, it seems insane to waste so much time so casually here.

But let's first talk more generally about using the controls, and then come to brakes and steering in more detail.

2.8.1 Using the controls

> **Key point**: - **Superior control comes from using the controls naturally.**

This will be controversial, but it is unfortunate that so many of the hot debates in driver training over the years have concentrated on precise ways to use the controls - even after the early stages of learning. With some of them, it is difficult for experienced drivers to see that they are necessary to the goal of full and reliable control. An example is steering technique which is discussed below, and there are more.

The aim in learning to use the controls is to master them to the extent that they become fully automatic responses to what you want the car to do. Most of your physical actions should fade into the background, so that your attention is:

> focused almost totally on what is happening
> <u>outside</u> the car, rather than <u>inside</u> it.

At higher levels of skill, control over the car comes increasingly from the closeness between driver and machine. At expert level, the car has become a full extension of the body. The driver knows exactly its capabilities and how it will respond. Some trainers teach this as:

> "The car is you, you are the car".

At this point, all of the controls are used naturally and precisely, and whenever they are needed in any situation. And always under full and reliable control.

Actions are not determined by preset rules or procedures, but only by experienced judgement about what is necessary at the time. This gives far superior car control. In the same way, you don't need to be told which muscles to operate when you walk. It would be unnecessary and obstructive to what you do very well naturally.

This means that the expert driver will, for example, use more steering techniques than the basic push-pull method (see later), may change gear while braking if it feels right, and will brake on a bend if necessary - but gently and knowing the effects on grip. Rather than "driving a car", this is just "driving" - driver and machine as one.

However, you should especially:

> be careful of trying to do too much at the same time.

In a safe situation, you may for example, cope with very light steering and gentle braking while also changing gear. But it is easy to overload your actions when hazards are around. And this happens easily with the hands if the mix is complicated by things like fiddling with the sound system or winding a window at the wrong time. If there is any hint of conflict, you should decide to separate the actions into a calm and unhurried sequence.

Your focus should always be on achieving:

> full and reliable control with totally natural use of the controls.

2.8.2 Braking

For most of us, braking just means pressing the pedal. And we usually hover our right foot over the accelerator until we decide to do it. But this habit creates braking that is later and heavier than it needs to be. A "softer and earlier" action will reduce risk.

A lot depends on how you think about braking, and it can help to see three stages.

The first two are often not considered at all:

1. engine braking
2. covering the brake pedal
3. pressing the pedal

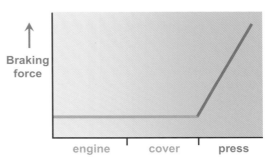

Engine braking

We could call this "passive" braking, since it happens by simply releasing the throttle. Perhaps it is sometimes just the moment while your foot is taken off the throttle and dropped on to the brake, and then back again in a jerky "go-stop-go" fashion.

It is better practice to:

> use engine braking more actively.

Although it is relatively gentle, with good anticipation this will shed speed quite well. And it gives a smoother and calmer drive. It also creates less disturbance for the traffic behind too, because you are more predictable.

That is, of course, not to discourage you from using the brake pedal when you need it! But the aim should be to gradually need it a bit less.

In fact:

> how much unplanned braking you need
> is a measure of your standard of anticipation.

Covering the brake pedal

This is a vital step, and where a lot of time can be gained. It means moving the right foot to the brake as soon as you suspect you <u>may</u> need to brake - not waiting to be sure that you must.

And the foot should <u>touch</u> the pedal, not be held above it. This is very powerful as both physical and mental preparation.

By touching the pedal:

the foot is ready to act,

quickly and accurately with whatever pressure is needed, without having to stab at it.

Also, mentally, you are far more likely to start braking "soft and early" if your foot is already there.

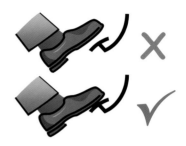

Notice again, the link to your anticipation skill that detects at an early stage when the need to brake is emerging.

You should:

**consider covering the brake when driving
towards or through most threats,**

such as brake lights ahead, passing busy side roads, approaching a blind bend or brow, children on the footpath, hidden driveways, and so on.

If your foot stays above the accelerator until after your decision to brake:

you can easily lose 1-2 seconds

in the physical and mental effects combined. And in a crisis, even one second of maximum braking can take about 20mph off your speed!

Pressing the pedal

This part you already know. It ranges from a gentle pressure that finely tunes the speed, up to full panic action to escape an impact. But:

over-use of braking is a very common style,

which again, is part of being "late and heavy". Under normal conditions, this pedal should be used with as much delicate finesse as the other controls.

Having said that, it is also true, as discussed before, that the ability to brake heavily and safely is a neglected skill too.

Don't forget that most crashes involve a failed emergency stop.

A terrific advance in braking ability has been achieved with ABS - but only if used properly. There are three common mistakes to avoid - all potential life-saving points. The first two have been blamed for drivers with ABS having perversely <u>higher</u> crash rates.

But they are all problems with the driver, rather than the system itself:

- Because braking needs less pedal pressure compared to non-ABS brakes, it inspires overconfidence in stopping ability, and tempts drivers to rely on heavier braking.

- It is common to release the pedal pressure when the ABS kicks-in and makes it vibrate, because it feels as if something has broken. Pressure must be kept full on. You should also <u>not</u> try to use cadence braking techniques to maintain grip, because that is exactly what the system does, but faster.

- The instinct to "freeze" the wheel under heavy braking means that evasive action is not taken when it was probably possible. So drivers fail to steer around their obstacle - even though the car could do so. They have no experience of being able to do this with the brakes fully on. And drivers are still told not to brake and steer at the same time, with "do not brake in a bend".

Ford coined the phrase "Step, Stay, Steer" to explain how to use ABS. But it is crucial to understand that ABS cannot work miracles by creating more grip than the surface has. And it also does little to improve dry road braking. Its main advantage comes in preventing wheel-lock to maintain steering control and improve braking on wet or icy surfaces.

The advent of ABS, therefore, makes it even more worth finding a training event to make sure you can safely apply maximum braking - and controlled swerving too. This will:

let your brain "prove" to itself what is possible,

and will begin to alter previous instincts. But even at training events, some drivers are reluctant to invoke the ABS - not liking the thought of the pedal vibrating under their foot.

Also in braking, it is best to avoid the exotic techniques like left-foot braking or heel-and-toe, that are sometimes used by racing drivers. They are not necessary for public road driving, and are likely to confuse your instinctive responses.

2.8.3 Steering

> Key points: - A sloppy grip on the wheel can lose you 2-3
> seconds in taking evasive action.
>
> - Using a variety of steering methods is not bad
> practice, provided you have absolute control.

This control is in constant use, and steering techniques have always been closely scrutinised during any training. Most drivers, though, probably believe they have pretty good steering skills - at least going forwards.

Thanks mainly to power assistance, modern cars have much lighter steering than a few decades ago. And it is also higher geared, so needs less turning of the wheel. But being easier to use can also open new temptations to treat it more casually.

There are two parts to your steering:

how you hold the wheel, and how you turn it.

And it is easy to become sloppy with them both. The overriding requirement remains to have total control at all times - including in a crisis.

Holding the wheel

This often receives less attention than the technique for turning the wheel, but is, in fact, more vital for control in most emergencies that occur.

As you watch other drivers, notice how many would be totally unable to react to a sudden surprise in front of them:

because they have such a poor grip on the wheel.

Typically over 80% of drivers handicap themselves in this way. Imagine them having to do a rapid zigzig manoeuvre to avoid the vehicle in front, and still be in perfect control. A one-handed grip is very common, as also is just flopping a hand over the top or bottom of the wheel. You will see drivers who use the wheel as an object to lean on - there are endless variations. And they happily drive like this into high risk situations, as if the angels had marked them for special protection.

Often it is worse on long journeys and the bigger roads, where people settle into their driving and get "really comfortable".

But:

recovering from a sloppy grip to one capable of robust and controlled action can take 2-3 seconds.

Even assuming that the hands still know what a good grip is. By which time fate will have already played its hand.

Unfortunately, "sloppy grip on the wheel" will not be listed as causing the crash. It cannot be proved, and no one would own up to it! Instead something else is blamed, and little is learned.

Traditionally, we have been taught to use the "10-to-2" hold, which is good.

It gets both hands on the wheel, and is fairly well balanced for taking action.

But it can be:

even better to drop slightly to the "quarter-to-three" position,

which is increasingly favoured by many trainers and experienced drivers.

Being slightly lower it is less tiring on long journeys, but more importantly, it is perfectly balanced about the centre of the wheel. It is therefore an ideal grip for taking very robust and accurate evasive action - without having to tense the body as a counter-weight.

A good hold also gives far better feedback from the front wheels about what the car is doing.

On the negative side, beware of "hand distractions", such as holding a cigarette, a phone, a sandwich, or anything else that takes a hand from the wheel. This is far more likely to make you fumble the steering if done at the wrong time. Even gear changes should be timed to make sure that the hand is available to do it.

Turning the wheel

There are many ways to turn a steering wheel, especially since power steering has removed the need for brute force. They include: push-pull, fixed grip, overhand rotation, underhand sweep, palming... and many more variations.

Without being aware of what they do, the vast majority of drivers use a number of techniques, to fit the circumstances. And:

there is no single way that is right and safest for all situations.

But the priority must still always be about having full and reliable control. Your comfort in making the movements is also a factor, but a secondary one.

Whether your own technique contains bad habits that sacrifice good control is hard for a book to tell! You need to assess for yourself how smoothly and accurately you are moving the wheel, and how easily you could be caught out if something unexpected happened.

"Push-pull" steering method

Certainly, the traditional mandate to use only the push-pull method is misplaced. It does help early drivers to avoid getting their arms tangled up when the wheel is still an alien object. But after that it is controversial, and has been heavily criticised for no longer meeting the needs of modern driving, amid safety concerns that include:

- It can involve a lot of rapid arm movements, with an alternating grip between the hands, and because of this it has been dubbed the "shuffle".

- It is comparatively slow unless expertly executed.

"Fixed grip" steering

In this method, both hands remain firmly gripping the wheel, typically in the quarter-to-three hold, as it is turned round and back again to straight - even if one hand goes a little over the top on the turn.

This gives an extremely secure, smooth and precise control, even when used rapidly and robustly for evasive action. You also know exactly where the straight ahead position of the wheel is, instantly and with absolute certainty.

This grip copes well with most circumstances, except when more movement is needed for tight turns.

The "rotational" method

When more turning is needed, the rotational method can be used.

Here your hand goes up and far over the top of the wheel and down the other side, to be followed by the other hand in a rolling motion. It allows very rapid turning. As with push-pull, it involves an alternating one-handed grip on the wheel, but to a lesser extent.

Its use is mainly for slow speed tight turns where there is also no need for absolute precision. (It is also used when lots of rapid steering is needed in high speed handling manoeuvres, but these are a specialised area).

In practice, you may find that the choice of steering methods is also dependent on the size of the steering wheel, the vehicle's turning circle and the number of turns lock-to-lock. Imagine adopting the push-pull or fixed grip method on a five-and-a-half turn lock-to-lock vehicle!

Whichever steering method you are using for your situation, though (except reversing), sitting with your back firmly against the seat will give a good anchor for your action. Drivers who sit forward off the seat - usually the more nervous ones - will find themselves either tensing around the stomach or using the wheel to hold themselves in position. And this will sacrifice control.

In closing

We set out at the beginning to dramatically increase the control that <u>you have</u> over the dangers that you will inevitably face on modern roads - especially those caused by other people. I hope your reading has been an absorbing and valuable journey - and one that you will refer back to at times.

Recall that the approach in **Mind Driving** is unique. By focusing directly on your <u>thinking</u> it improves how you <u>make the decisions</u> which will <u>actively manage the risk</u>. This is different to traditional teaching, and opens a more effective route to safe driving.

The journey has, therefore, ventured far beyond the basic "hands-and-feet" ability, and has unravelled the "<u>eyes-and-brain</u>" skills that are the real key to controlling danger.

In working through the book, you have travelled through two important stages.

The first was Part 1: **Defining the Skills**. This explained the process of driving in a completely new way, that has a very clear and powerful structure.

And by doing this we revealed a set of eight specific skills that define what we need to be good at. They work together, and anyone can learn them.

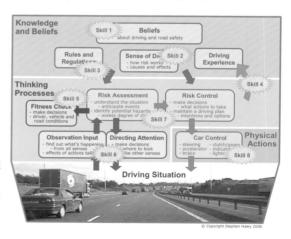

Then the second step, in Part 2: **Gaining the Skills**, is the main part of the book, and described each of the eight essential skills in detail.

The most extensive coverage was given to the skills that are not already imparted through traditional driver training.

Summarising the skills again, they are:

Knowledge and Beliefs	1. **Beliefs**	Ten simple beliefs that will make you noticeably safer.
	2. **Sense of Danger**	Three causes of danger, to be kept in balance - Speed, Surprise and Space.
	3. **Rules and Regulations**	Rules of the road are essential, but they cannot guarantee your safety.
Thinking Processes	4. Learning from Experience	The engine of all your skills, and a vital skill in itself.
	5. **Fitness Check**	Clear decisions about whether you should be driving at all.
	6. **Observation**	Making sure you notice and understand what is important, and at the right time.
	7. **Risk Assessment and Control**	Directly controlling the root causes of danger - to actively keep risk low.
Physical Actions	8. **Car Control**	Saving crucial seconds in braking and steering techniques.

Remember, though, that a book can only do so much. What you really achieve will always depend on what you do out on the road - improving skills and keeping them honed sharp. It will always be true that:

your skills <u>are</u> how you drive.

Recall too, as your skills develop, that building a good process of learning is as vital as the knowledge and techniques that you gain. This is the key to a true life-skill.

And lastly, the sincere hope is that this new approach will genuinely become:

"the driving skills you can live by".

Enjoy a long and safe motoring career!

Acknowledgements

It would be a rare book indeed that is written without help. And this one is no exception.

I am deeply indebted to the following people and thank them warmly for their diverse influence, support and encouragement, especially in the early and formative stages of the project:

- Kevin Delaney, Andrew Howard, Mark McArthur-Christie, Paul Smith, Pete Garvey, Adrian Shurmer, members of the workshop in October 2004 and the multitude of the wider "team" - for letting me intrude into their busy schedules, and whose enthusiasm for the project spurred me on.
- Nick Keith - for so effortlessly pointing me towards a much better writing style, though he might not know that he did. Phil Kay - for helping me through some interesting technical problems. And everyone else at the Ecademy Writers Club who also gave their support.
- All the people around the world who gave such positive feedback to the Skilldriver.org website in early 2005, which contained the initial online book.
- My son, Paul, who at the end of 2004 calmly took the skills of this impatient student from zero to having the whole book and project loaded on to a working website in just 6 weeks - and all in raw html code.
- My family - wife, son, daughter and mother (yes, she was roped in too!) - for not only giving the obsession a lot of space and time in the clamour of family life, but also reading and discussing the endless stream of disjointed pages that rolled off the printer.

Without them this book would be still just churning in my head.

Stephen Haley

Good Driver?

Mind Driving identifies the skills and techniques to help you to become a better driver. But how good a driver are you already? And how do you go about objectively measuring your current level of ability?

The easiest way is to take an advanced driving test.

A number of organisations offer advanced tests, including DIAmond Advanced Motorists, the IAM (Institute of Advanced Motorists) and RoSPA. Although different in format and content, all three have the ultimate aim of improving a candidate's driving skill and thereby benefiting road safety.

However, the DIAmond Advanced Test, introduced in 1992, is the only one to use the Government Driving Standards Agency's own test marking system - the prestigious Cardington system used to test the ability of driver trainers. This brings the test up to date with the latest developments in the L-test, and then applies a more exacting standard to ensure the highest level of driving practice.

There are actually two tests, the DIAmond Advanced Test and DIAmond Special Test. The latter is currently the most stringent measure of driving ability available in the UK, and both are also available to motorcyclists.

All drivers should periodically undergo some sort of driving assessment. Whilst particularly crucial for vocational drivers (more so than ever under current health and safety regulations), all motorists, irrespective of their work, should prove themselves responsible road users by putting themselves to the test.

You may be a good driver, but are you a DIAmond driver?

Prove it by putting yourself to the test.

PROVE IT!

For further information on DIAmond Advanced Motorists or Motorcyclists, please telephone DIAmond on 0845 345 5151 or, for international callers, +44 208 665 5151.

DIAmond Advanced Motorists is part of the Safety House group.

About Safety House

Safety House has its headquarters in Croydon, Greater London, and brings together road safety professionals, driver trainers, advanced drivers, advanced motorcyclists and academic experts from all over the world.

Its purpose is to help reduce road casualties by promoting higher standards of driver training and road safety. And to do this across a broad range of activities that have developed around the DIA, the largest organisation representing professional driver trainers throughout the UK.

Organisations under the Safety House banner include:

DIA - the Driving Instructors Association

> The largest professional association for driver trainers in the UK

DIAmond Advanced Motorists

> Providing objective advanced driving and motorcycling assessments to businesses and individuals

IVV - International Association for Driver Education
(Internationaler Verband für Verkehrserziehung)

> The IVV was founded fifty years ago, and is the only worldwide association representing the interests of those involved in furthering education in road safety

IRSTE - Institute of Road Safety Training Executives

> The professional association for owners, managers and senior individuals within the road safety industry

DERF - Driver Education Research Foundation

> Providers of academic research in the road safety industry

Driving Instructor Accident and Disability Fund

> Charity providing assistance to teachers of driving and their families who have met unfortunate circumstances

SAFEX

World road safety conferences held every two years throughout the world

DRIVEX

Exhibitions and ride and drive events

Driving Instructor

The voice of the driver training industry

Driving Magazine

For advanced drivers and road safety professionals.

For more information:

Safety House, Beddington Farm Road, Croydon CR0 4XZ
Tel 0845 345 5151   Fax 020 8665 5565

For international enquiries:
Tel +44 208 665 5151   Fax +44 208 665 5565

safetyhouse@driving.org   www.driving.org